American Politics, Then & Now
and Other Essays

American Politics, Then & Now
and Other Essays

James Q. Wilson

The AEI Press

Publisher for the American Enterprise Institute

WASHINGTON, D.C.

Distributed to the Trade by National Book Network, 15200 NBN Way, Blue Ridge Summit, PA 17214. To order call toll free 1-800-462-6420 or 1-717-794-3800. For all other inquiries please contact the AEI Press, 1150 Seventeenth Street, N.W., Washington, D.C. 20036 or call 1-800-862-5801.

Library of Congress Cataloging-in-Publication Data

Wilson, James Q.
  American politics, then & now and other essays / James Q. Wilson.
    p. cm.
  Includes index.
  ISBN-13: 978-0-8447-4319-6 (hardcover)
  ISBN-10: 0-8447-4319-4 (hardcover)
  1. United States—Politics and government—1989–2. United
States—Politics and government—1945–1989. I. Title.
  JK275.W55 2010
  320.973—dc22

                                                              2010002626

14 13 12 11 10   1 2 3 4 5

Printed in the United States of America

Contents

Acknowledgments

I am grateful to Arthur Brooks for allowing me to publish these essays in an AEI book, and for the excellent editorial help I have had from Laura Harbold, Anne Himmelfarb, and Sam Thernstrom. Karlyn Bowman at AEI was a valuable coauthor of an essay reprinted here. I also want to acknowledge my great indebtedness to the journals that have published my essays over many years: *Commentary*, *City Journal*, *The Public Interest*, and *National Affairs*. Robert Faulkner and Susan Shell published my essay on religion and politics in their book, *America at Risk* (University of Michigan Press, 2009). Much of my work has been supported by the Earhart, Sloan, and Tanner foundations.

Preface

These essays, written over a thirty-year period, are my account of how American politics, and the world in which America's political system operates, have changed. These changes have been fundamental. The American government does not make decisions today the way it made them in the 1950s or during the New Deal era in the 1930s. Familiar institutions have been weakened or destroyed, replaced by a commitment to ideas and ideologies the consequences of which we do not fully understand.

Franklin Roosevelt led the country during the first hundred days of his administration with policies that were new, but he worked in a political system that had not changed much for about a century. Seventy-six years later, the press celebrated Barack Obama's first hundred days with accounts of all that he had attempted, and without comment on the new political order of which they were a part. Nobody in 1933 knew whether FDR's new policies would work; today nobody knows whether Obama's will work, either. But our political system has changed so dramatically that the current economic recession, one vastly less serious than what greeted FDR, has permitted Obama to attempt to nationalize parts of the auto industry, hire and fire bank managers, and set in motion a plan that may, in effect, nationalize our health care system.

In his first term FDR created a bank holiday to stop a run on banks, devised an insurance scheme to provide welfare benefits to the elderly, did not attempt to do much about health care, and in the teeth of some public hostility created unemployment benefits and Aid to Families with Dependent Children, which would be administered by the states. The more leftist supporters of the New Deal wanted to create an American social democracy, but had to settle instead for an American state: that is, a sense of national identity managed by a national government to achieve national purposes. The Supreme Court, after initial resistance, approved of this new direction. The Second World War reinforced America's sense of itself as a nation with a powerful central government that would impose high taxes. And the war did what the New Deal did not: it ended the Depression.

The determination to create a social democracy was reborn with the advent of Barack Obama to the presidency. In his first few months in office, Obama ordered the merger or abolition of several banks, passed out stimulus checks directly to the people, gave money to the auto companies (on the condition that one company get rid of its chief executive officer and that all make the kinds of cars federal officials liked), and called for a federal health plan that would "compete with" (which may mean replace) private health plans. In a government-managed program to help people buy insurance and to manage the prices doctors charge, there will be federal subsidies that permit the plan to price its services below those of private health-care plans, thus driving many out of business. By this means we may move toward a "single-payer" (i.e., government-only) health program, thereby bringing to this country the defects of such plans that are so visible in Canada and Great Britain.

All of this is hard to believe at a time when the economy is in a deep recession and the public wants the government to do what it can to end it. The government, both under George W. Bush and Barack Obama, has tried with, I think, mixed effects. But what is astonishing is that the Obama administration has promised no higher taxes for the middle class when its health care plan will raise taxes and its cap-and-trade environmental plan will raise fuel costs. In 1933 matters were very different: the public wanted an end to the Depression and the FDR administration worked, again with mixed effects, to do that. The magnitude of the changes in public policy between 1933 and 2009 is, to my mind, a measure of the changes in how this country is governed. To be sure, the New Deal had brought about, in Morton Keller's words, a "sea change in American public life." But to believers in a Western European model of democracy, much was left to be done.[1] What was impossible or difficult in the first period has become reasonable and even easy in the second.

In part this change has to do with the rise of strict party-line votes. Before the health care plan was adopted in 2010 with every Republican opposed and almost every Democrat in favor, the three most important pieces of legislation in the twentieth century had bipartisan support: Social Security was passed in 1935 with fifteen House Republicans and five Senate Republicans in favor of it; the Civil Rights Act of 1964 was passed with sixty-four House Republicans and six Senate Republicans in favor; and Medicare was passed in 1965 with sixty-five House Republicans and thirteen Senate Republicans in favor.

In part it has to do with the extent to which the government today acts with indifference to public opinion. The pending passage of the health care bill makes this clear as well. Only one-third of the public favors the plan that Congress has adopted, and the Speaker of the House declared that she was willing for her party to lose forty seats in the next election in order to do what she, but not the voters, thought was important.

Liberals celebrate this new level of vigor and intrusiveness in national policymaking, and conservatives regret it; but whichever group's judgment proves correct, the fact of the change indicates that our political system today is not what James Madison, Woodrow Wilson, or even Harry Truman would have recognized. The chief mystery of contemporary politics is how such a fundamental change was possible; the essays that follow examine this mystery and try to explain it.

It is all the more important to understand this transformation because it is occurring at a time when the United States is deeply but reluctantly engaged with the rest of the world. At one time our policy was to shun the rest of the world; at a later time it was to mobilize to confront well-known national enemies, such as the German Kaiser, Adolf Hitler, and Joseph Stalin. When we shunned the world, Americans liked that; when we fought national enemies, Americans were united behind the effort. But today, when we try to cope with struggles in Afghanistan and Iraq, our leaders discover that they must cope both with allies who dislike them and Americans who oppose them—just as they did when we fought in Vietnam. The peace party—as Karlyn Bowman and I showed using poll data—is about one-fifth of the American public, and has been that for almost half a century.

The foreign enemies with whom we now struggle are composed not of hostile nations but of stateless radicals driven by what they take to be (wrongly, in my view) the requirements of deeply held religious beliefs. It is a bitter paradox: America, the most religious of all advanced nations, must fight against the distorted religion of certain radicalized people. America had managed, with some difficulty, to reconcile religious beliefs and personal freedom only to discover that it must contend with people for whom religion and freedom are irreconcilably opposed. And in between this country and its enemies lies Western Europe, where freedom has been acquired by downgrading or destroying religion.

Americans fight because they value life and freedom, whereas the jihadists fight because they value death and submission. The tactics necessary to cope with that struggle were slow to develop in the American military and not given a clear written statement until General David Petraeus and his colleagues produced the Army–Marine Corps manual on counterinsurgency, which became something of a best seller in 2007. Its message did not simply outline a new tactic; it called for the American military to rethink its central doctrines. No one should be surprised to learn that the American public now cherishes our military and distrusts Congress and the mass media. After all, the military has improved, and (I argue) Congress and the media have become worse.

Some readers will take these essays as the grumpy words of a conservative who can't be reconciled to the realities of contemporary American life. Maybe. But they are also meant to be a warning to our leaders, who when they pursue liberal goals must not lose sight of or throw away what is exceptional about America. Americans, starting with the New Deal, began to expect a lot from Washington, but they did not learn to love the policymakers who work there. Americans worry about opportunity, but they do not distrust economic inequality provided such differences have been fairly earned. Americans want problems solved, but they also cherish personal freedom. Americans feel that they are not simply residents in a certain nation but participants in a particular creed; unlike most Europeans, they feel that they have a special inheritance that values future accomplishments. The task facing policymakers is to do reasonable things to manage problems while leaving intact America's remarkable commitment to the prospect of human growth that is purchased not only by making decisions but also by taking risks.

The essays in this volume are divided into three sections. The first set of essays discusses how our politics has changed, and how our people and our Congress have become more polarized. The second reflects on religion and freedom; the essays look specifically at religion as a polarizing force in the United States and at Islam's failure to reconcile religion with individual autonomy. The third section explores the implications of the newest research on genes and heredity for our political beliefs, our understanding of human character, and our most basic notions of freedom.

A few changes have been made in these essays since they were first published.[2] I have deleted some things that no longer interest anyone, and have dropped a passage or two where experience has shown that I was wrong. The leading example was my skepticism, expressed in the 1970s, about the feasibility of an all-volunteer military force. I was wrong about that, though it is conceivable (but I hope unlikely) that our future military requirements may make conscription once again necessary. I have also added a brief introduction to each essay, mainly reflecting on what has changed since I first wrote the piece, and on whether the trends I identified have continued or fizzled.

JAMES Q. WILSON, May 2010

Notes

1. Morton Keller, *America's Three Regimes: A New Political History* (New York: Oxford University Press, 2007), 209.

2. One aspect of the essays that has not changed is their documentation. A few of the essays when first published included documentary notes, and these notes are retained in this volume; for the essays first published without notes (the majority), no notes have been added.

PART I

The Changing Nature of American Politics

1

American Politics, Then & Now
Originally published in Commentary, February 1979

This essay was written after Lyndon Johnson, Richard Nixon, and Jimmy Carter had been president. It describes how American politics has changed since an earlier era, when bipartisan support was the basis for most new legislation. In 1970, only one-quarter of House votes pitted a majority of Democrats against a majority of Republicans; in 2002, nearly one-half of House votes were of this kind. Perhaps as a result, there has been a sharp drop in the number of bills passed by Congress (941 in 1970, but only 383 in 2002). Much of this change was the result of each party becoming ideologically more coherent: the Democrats were overwhelmingly liberal, the Republicans just as completely conservative.

———❦———

In 1948, the late John Fischer published in *Harper's* magazine an article entitled "Unwritten Rules of American Politics," which was at the time, and for many years thereafter, widely recognized as the best brief analysis of the distinctive features of American politics. He drew upon the writings of John C. Calhoun, the South Carolina politician and intellectual who nearly a century before had set forth the doctrine of the "concurrent majority." In Calhoun's time, of course, that doctrine was a defense of the southern resistance to federal legislation aimed at restricting the spread of slavery, but Fischer, aided by the writings of Peter Drucker, found that if one stripped the theory of the concurrent majority of its extremist and partisan language, it offered an enduring and fundamental explanation of the American constitutional system.

That system was designed to preserve liberty and maintain a national union by ensuring that no important decision would be reached without the concurrence of each interest vitally affected by that decision. In Congress, no important bloc would be voted down on any matter that touched its central concern. In nominating a presidential candidate, no one would be acceptable who was objectionable to any significant body of opinion within the party. In electing a president, both parties would sacrifice any interest in principle or policy to accommodate the views of the average voter and thus would almost always offer an echo, not a choice. Politics would be nonideological, conflict would be minimized, and such policies as survived the process of interest-group bargaining would command widespread support and thus be likely to endure. All these were, to Fischer, the strengths of the system. It had costs as well—a disposition to inaction, a tendency to magnify the power of well-organized pressure groups, and a shortage of persons able to speak for the nation as a whole. But to Fischer, the strengths clearly outweighed the weaknesses, primarily because man is fallible: the very slowness of the system insured against the premature commitment to error. As Learned Hand once wrote, "The spirit of liberty is the spirit which is not too sure that it is right."

Fischer's concern for moderation, even at the price of inaction, was under-standable in its time. In 1948, the Democratic Party was split into three wings. Progressives (and the Communist Party) were supporting Henry Wallace, and southern reactionaries were supporting Strom Thurmond, while beleaguered Harry Truman was struggling—as it turned out, successfully—to hold the Democratic middle.

Persons who believe that the American system as Fischer understood it has changed point to the legislative explosion that occurred during the 1960s and early 1970s. Without benefit of a national emergency, which in the past had always been necessary for the system of veto groups to be set aside, there poured forth from Congress an unprecedented wave of policy innovation. The southern filibuster was broken and civil rights bills became law. The caution of the House Ways and Means Committee was overcome and Medicare and Medicaid were passed. The fear of federal control of schools that had long prevented federal aid to education were set aside, and such aid became a massive and growing reality. The War on Poverty, the Model Cities Program, and the rest of the Great Society legislation arrived, to be followed, toward the end of the 1960s, by the emergence of environmental and consumer legislation. Between 1966 and 1970, Congress passed at least eighteen major consumer protection laws and seven major laws limiting air and water pollution laws, and the activity continued well into the 1970s.

As important as the number of new programs adopted was the way in which they were adopted. The veto groups and congressional blocs that were thought to stand astride each checkpoint in the legislative process, letting nothing pass without first extracting every necessary concession, were scarcely to be found. The bill creating federal aid to education went through committee review and floor debate virtually without amendment, leading three Republicans on a House subcommittee to boycott the hearings on the bill because of the "hasty and superficial consideration" it was receiving. The original Medicare plan would have paid just the hospital bills of the elderly; Congress added a provision for public payment of doctors' bills as well. Congressional deliberations on the auto safety bill of 1966 made that law, in virtually every particular, stronger than what the president had requested; when the conference committee considered the versions passed by the House and Senate, it resolved all remaining issues in favor of the tougher— that is, the more anti-industry—provisions. By the end of the 1960s, the American Medical Association, long described as one of the most powerful interest groups in Washington, had been defeated, the automobile industry stood revealed (in Elizabeth Drew's phrase) as a "paper hippopotamus," and Ralph Nader had become the best-known and perhaps the most powerful lobbyist in town.

A Real Change?

The opposite view is that, despite the frenzy of the 1960s, nothing of fundamental importance changed. The Carter presidency has been functioning rather like the Truman presidency: unheroically, with little public enthusiasm, winning some battles and losing others. Not only were liberal ideas, such as civil rights, national health insurance, and federal aid to education, defeated in 1948, they were ignored or defeated in the 1970s. Though the nation was at peace in 1948 as in 1976, both presidents were preoccupied in large measure with foreign affairs—the Marshall Plan, NATO, and international trade in the case of Truman, the Panama Canal, the Middle East, and Turkey in the case of Carter. Both presidents saw Congress debate at length a bill to deregulate natural gas, and neither president was able to get out of the debate exactly what he wanted. Truman vetoed a deregulation bill passed in 1950, Carter signed a compromise deregulation bill in 1978. During his first year in office, Carter won on 75 percent of the congressional votes taken on his program, a level of support far lower than that enjoyed by Eisenhower, Kennedy, and Johnson in their first or second years.

The conservative coalition of Republicans and southern Democrats which has been the bane of liberal legislation was, according to the *Congressional Quarterly*, alive and well in the ninety-fifth Congress. During 1977, it appeared in about one-fourth of the recorded votes in the House and Senate and won about two-thirds of the time that it appeared. Truman would not have been surprised.

The burst of legislation in the 1960s was not the result, in this skeptical view, of any profound change in American politics, but was simply a consequence of the Goldwater fiasco. The Lyndon Johnson victory in 1964 gave the Democrats so large a majority in Congress that northern Democratic liberals acquired a control of Congress that formerly only a national crisis would produce. Northern Democrats could have passed the aid-to-education bill and come within a few votes of passing the Medicare bill even if every Republican and southern Democrat had voted against them. Moreover, the Goldwater candidacy brought Republicans to power in parts of the South and thereby reduced the control that southerners, by virtue of the seniority system, had once wielded in Congress. In 1962, Alabama had eight Democratic congressmen; after 1964, only three were left.

But with the 1970s, normalcy returned, and with it either (depending on one's political convictions) stagnation or prudence. The struggle over the energy bill was mountainous, and yet what the mountain brought forth was not even a mouse, but a Tinker Toy out of which a gifted administrator might be able to fashion a reasonable facsimile of a mouse. Congress has reasserted its influence over foreign affairs, in part by the enactment of five or six dozen provisions in foreign aid and other laws requiring congressional assent to presidential initiatives. Whatever vision one has of a fair and rational tax code, there seems little prospect of Congress transforming that vision into reality.

In short, once extraordinary majorities evaporate and national crises recede, it is politics as usual. Recently, Senator Edward M. Kennedy attacked

Congress for being "the best money could buy" and criticized the profusion and influence of interest groups. Though Kennedy was deploring what Fischer had applauded, the categories of description were very much the same.

The Expansion of the Political Agenda

Both interpretations of American politics are partially correct. Congress remains able, long after the 1960s, to pass sweeping new laws almost without regard to the normal constraints of interest-group bargaining, as it did when it decided in 1978 to abolish mandatory retirement before age seventy or in 1973 to give absolute protection to endangered species. And Congress continues to experience great difficulty in formulating a coherent policy on matters such as taxation, energy, or school desegregation. As Anthony King has observed, our political system has acquired the contradictory tendencies of a human crowd—"to move either very sluggishly or with extreme speed."[1]

Three things account for the schizophrenia of contemporary politics: one is the greater ease with which decisions can be transferred from the private to the public sphere; a second is the "atomization," as King terms it, of political institutions; a third is a change in the governing ideas of our time. The first factor has caused the American law-making system to be in a state of permanent excitability; the second has made the outcome of any excitement difficult to predict; and the third has been the source of the energy that determines whether the system will be in its manic or depressive phase.

Madison and the other framers of the Constitution, as everyone knows, sought to prevent the mischief of faction and the tyranny of temporary majorities by so arranging the federal government's institutions that ambition would be made to check ambition. Douglass C. North, the economic historian, has stated one consequence of the Madisonian system this way: in order to reduce the ability of interest groups to capture the government, the constitutional order attached a high cost to utilizing the political system as compared to the marketplace for making decisions. The entry price for politics was high, and thus only the largest or most popular factions were able to pay it. This price was both tangible and intangible. The material cost was the great effort required to organize groups (parties, factions, lobbies) influential enough to get an issue onto the agenda of Congress and to coordinate the decision of Congress (and its many parts) and the president. The nonmaterial cost was the widespread belief that a large range of issues—public welfare, civil rights, the regulation of economic enterprise, even for a while the building of public works—was outside the legitimate scope of federal authority.

The late E. E. Schattschneider once observed that "he who decides what politics is about runs the country." Once politics was about only a few things; today, it is about nearly everything. There has been, in North's terms, a "drastic reduction in the cost of using the political process" relative to the cost of using, for similar results, the market. That reduction has been the result of easier access to the courts (by fee shifting and class-action suits), the greater ease of financing interest groups with foundation grants and direct-mail fund-raising, and the multiplication of government agencies and congressional staffs.

Not only have the money costs of using political strategies fallen; the ideological costs have declined as well. Until rather recently, the chief issue in any congressional argument over new policies was whether it was legitimate for the federal government to do something at all. That was the crux of the dispute over Social Security, welfare, Medicare, civil rights, selective service, foreign aid, international alliances, price and wage controls, economic regulation, and countless other departures from the past. But once the initial law is passed, the issue of legitimacy disappears, and, except in those few cases where the Supreme Court later holds the law unconstitutional, does not reemerge.

Once the legitimacy barrier has fallen, political conflict takes a very different form. New programs need not await the advent of a crisis or an extraordinary majority, because no program is any longer "new"—it is seen, rather, as an extension, a modification, or an enlargement of something the government is already doing. Congressmen will argue about "how much," or "where," or "what kind," but not about "whether." One consequence is that the workload of Congress will grow astronomically.

Since there is virtually nothing the government has not tried to do, there is little it cannot be asked to do. Congressmen try frantically to keep up with this growing workload by adding to their staffs, but of course a bigger staff does not lead to less work, it leads to more, and so the ideas, demands, and commitments presented daily to a legislator grow even faster. Moreover,

Congress creates a bureaucracy of its own to keep up with the information-gathering and policy-generating capacities of the executive branch, leading to what Senator Daniel P. Moynihan has characterized as the "Iron Law of Emulation."[2]

This dramatic expansion of the political agenda has helped alter the distribution of political power. At one time, the legislative process was biased in favor of the opponents of any new policy. The committee system and the great powers of committee chairmen meant that the crucial calculation to be made by a proponent of a new policy was not how many congressmen were in favor of it, but which congressmen were opposed to it. The fact that the proposed policy was new and that there were few or no precedents for governmental action in that area made it easier for a Wilbur Mills, a James Eastland, or a Howard Smith to use his position on the House Ways and Means Committee, the Senate Judiciary Committee, or the House Rules Committee to block consideration of the proposal. But when the government is already doing something in the area, then there is an existing agency of government and its associated private supporters with a stake in the matter, and so actions will be taken to sustain, not criticize, the program.

Political scientists have frequently described American policymaking as "incremental." Some have used the term admiringly, because the process it describes builds consensus; others have used it critically, because that process prevents radical change and misrepresents some interests. But whatever one thinks of the concept, it is increasingly hard to believe it generally descriptive. We have brought under new regulatory machinery whole sectors of our economy; changed in one sudden blow the legality of a mandatory retirement age; rewritten (in a manner almost no one understands) the basic law governing retirement systems; banned the use of whole categories of chemicals; given to Congress a legislative veto over important parts of our foreign policy once reserved entirely for the president; adopted a vast and expensive system for financing health care; put under public auspices a large part of the American rail system; created public financing of presidential campaigns; changed the meaning of "equality of opportunity" from "fair competition" to "the achievement of racial goals"; and come close to authorizing cash grants to parents of children attending parochial schools and private colleges. These may be good ideas or they may be bad ones, but it is hard to describe them—and dozens of others like them—as "marginal" or "incremental" changes in policy.

The Atomization of Congress and the Parties

The second change that has taken place in contemporary politics is the atomization of certain key political institutions, notably Congress and the political parties. Congress has, to a degree, been deinstitutionalized and individualized: its leadership has become weaker, power within it has been dispersed, the autonomy and resources of its individual members have been enlarged. As a result, it is no longer helpful to think of Congress as consisting of blocs, each representing an interest group and each having a potential veto over measures affecting its vital interests. The weakening of congressional voting blocs might strike some readers as a gain: vested interests can no longer easily say no to things they oppose. But such a view neglects the price that has been paid for this change: if nobody can say no and make it stick, then nobody can say yes and make it stick. If there are no vetoes, neither are there any imprimaturs.

The individual member of Congress has gained enormously at the expense of committee chairmen, party leaders, and interest groups. He or she now has a large personal staff and a voice in the choice of the staff members of committees. (The congressional bureaucracy is probably the fastest-growing one in Washington, with no nonsense about civil service to inhibit it. By 1976 the staff was three times larger than it was in 1956.) The seniority system no longer governs the choice of committee chairmen to the exclusion of all other considerations; in 1975, House Democrats, by secret ballot, deposed three committee chairmen and elevated in their stead more junior members. Committees no longer regularly meet behind closed doors (whereas almost half of all House committee meetings were closed to the public in 1972, only 3 percent were by 1975).

Some of the enhanced autonomy and status of individual, especially junior, members of Congress was won by backbench revolts against leadership, but much of it was given to them by leaders attempting to build their own power by doing lasting favors for the rank and file. When Lyndon Johnson was Senate majority leader, his stature among freshmen senators was high in part because he adopted a practice in the 1950s of giving to each new senator at least one major committee assignment rather than, as had once been the case, making them wait patiently for the "club" to admit them into the ranks of the deserving. Among the latter-day beneficiaries of this generosity were George McGovern and Walter Mondale. In 1970, with only six years' seniority, McGovern became chairman of the Select Committee on Hunger, and Mondale, with only seven years of service, chairman of the Committee on School Segregation. The well-publicized hearings of these committees did not harm the political ambitions of their youthful chairmen. When Congress decentralizes power in order to enhance (temporarily) the authority of a given leader, the leader is acting much like the person who keeps his house warm in the winter by burning in the fireplace the furniture, the doors, and the walls. Soon there is nothing left to burn.

It is not just the formal apparatus of party and leadership in Congress that is weaker, but the informal and social organization as well. Not long after Fischer wrote, William White described the Senate "club" of veteran, chiefly southern, senators who dominated its affairs and acted, not surprisingly, entirely in the spirit of Calhoun and the concurrent majority. Within a decade after White wrote, the club was pretty much finished, the victim of deaths, retirements, defeats, and, above all, political change. In 1949, in the Congress elected when Fischer was writing, southerners held twice as many committee chairmanships as did northerners and westerners combined. By 1977, the southern committee chairman was the exception, not the rule. (By 2000, there was only one southern committee chairman.)

Individual members of Congress are far more secure in their seats than they were in the past, and with increased security goes increased freedom from those organizations, be they political parties or interest groups, that once controlled the resources necessary for reelection. Since 1960, there has been only one year when fewer than 90 percent of House incumbents were reelected. Moreover, of those running for reelection, fewer face close contests. When Fischer wrote in 1918, the winner of most House contests received 55 percent of the vote or less. By 1970, 60 per cent of the incumbents were reelected with at least 60 percent of the vote. Safe seats have become the rule, not the exception. Barring major electoral turnovers, such as in 1964, most new entrants to Congress come from those districts where incumbents have decided voluntarily to retire.

Campaign-finance laws will strengthen this pattern. By restricting individual donations initially to $1,000 and today to $2,000, they limit sharply the chances of unknown candidates with little personal wealth amassing large war chests to challenge well-known incumbents. By restricting donations from special-interest groups to $5,000, they limit the extent to which money can be the basis of group influence over legislators. (Rich candidates can still finance their own campaigns without restriction.)

The individualization and decentralization of Congress that have been the result of these changes in its internal affairs have been further augmented by the general decline of the political party, the increased use of radio and television for building personal followings in election campaigns, and the emergence of campaign organizations, often designed and staffed by professional campaign consultants, that are the personal property of the candidate rather than the collective effort of the party.

When Fischer wrote, presidential candidates were still picked by conventions in which party bosses were influential. In 1948 there were presidential primaries in only fourteen states, and in five of these unpledged delegations ran at large. The open party caucus was almost unheard of. Though the Democratic Party was deeply split among its ideological factions, the extremists of the left and right did not contest the primaries but organized instead as independent parties. President Truman had only nominal opposition at the 1948 convention but faced major rivals in the general election. But by the 1970s, there were primaries in most states and wide-open local caucuses in many others. In each party, the ideological divisions were obvious and wide. In 1948 party regularity was an important consideration for both convention delegates and presidential candidates; anybody who used such a term in 1976 would have elicited either a smile or a yawn. When compromises were made in 1948, they were intended to attract the middle-of-the-road voter; when they were made in 1976, their aim was to appease the more militant party activists (Walter Mondale was put on the Carter ticket to soothe the liberals, Robert Dole put on the Ford ticket to help please the conservatives).

All these factors have tended to make the Congress of today, in comparison with that about which Fischer wrote in 1948, a collection of individuals rather than blocs. More precisely, blocs exist, but they are typically formed by the members themselves, on the basis of personal political convictions or broad allegiances to regions or sectors of society, rather than in response to, or as an instrument of, an organized interest outside Congress. Perhaps the largest and most significant bloc today is the Democratic Study Group, an organization of liberal Democrats in the House. It has leaders, a staff, a budget, regular meetings; its influence is hard to measure but far from trivial. There is also a Black Caucus, and a Northeast-Midwest Economic Advancement Coalition. In 1948, congressmen were more likely to organize into a "farm bloc," or a "labor bloc," or an "oil bloc." Such influences still operate, of course, but groups based on ideology or racial or ethnic identification have become more important than those based on economic interest. And congressmen change their minds more frequently, making it harder to count in advance on their position.

The individualization of politics has meant that interest groups have had to individualize their appeal and link it directly to the electoral fortunes of individual members of Congress. Thus, the rise of grassroots lobbying—the careful, often computerized mobilization of letters, mailgrams, delegations, and financial contributions from individual citizens in each legislator's district or state. Mark Green, director of Ralph Nader's Congress Watch, said that grassroots lobbying has made Washington "an absolutely different city these days." Today, he noted, "you lose bills in the districts, not in Washington."

The Role of Ideas

But if key political institutions are becoming so atomized, how does any policy get passed? The explanation, I suspect, is to be found in the third change in politics I have alluded to—the enhanced importance of ideas and of ideology. To return to Anthony King's metaphor, what makes the difference between the sluggish and the rushing crowd is the force of a compelling idea.

The Congress today, much more than that of 1948, is susceptible to the power of ideas whenever there seems to be a strong consensus as to what the correct ideas are. Such a consensus existed in the mid-1960s about the Great Society legislation; no such consensus about these matters exists today. This helps explain, as Henry J. Aaron has noted, the changing prospects of social welfare policies. Consumer protection, ecology, campaign-finance reform, and congressional ethics are other examples of ideas with strong symbolic appeal that, so long as the consensus endures, are handled by a political process in which the advantage lies with the proponents of change.

When a consensus evaporates or a symbol loses its power, issues are handled by a process which, like that in 1948, gives the advantage to the opponents of change. But sooner or later, a scandal, a shift in the focus of media attention, or the efforts of a skilled policy entrepreneur will bring a compelling new idea to the top of the political agenda, and once again action will become imperative.

I do not wish to enter the argument about whether there has been an "end of ideology" in the West or whether there is a heightened degree of "ideological constraint" in the public at large. Within Congress, however, the Republican Party has become more consistently conservative and the Democratic Party more consistently liberal. Whatever has happened in society, the principle of affiliation among legislators has become more based on shared ideas, and to a degree those shared ideas conform to party labels. The notion of party in Congress has been infused with more ideological meaning by its members.

Much attention has rightly been paid to one source of politically influential ideas: the "New Class" composed of persons having high levels of education and professional occupations. This group is decidedly more liberal than other groups in society, so much so that Everett Ladd was able to conclude that by the early 1960s, a majority of the "privileged" elements in society considered themselves Democrats and voted for Democratic candidates for Congress. The New Class is responsive to, and provides support for, politicians who favor abortion on demand, environmental and consumer-protection laws, and equal rights for women. The liberalism of the professional class is illustrated by the fact that people who have graduate degrees are much more liberal than people who belong to labor unions.

Upper-middle-class white northern Protestants, once the bastion of traditional conservatism, have not been converted into a liberal New Class; they have been split into two deeply opposed groups. Sidney Verba and his co-workers found that in the 1950s, this group was the most conservative identifiable segment of American opinion. By the 1970s, however, a profound change had occurred—one part of this group had become even more conservative, while another part had become very liberal. High-status WASPs are now the most polarized class in America, and to the extent that this class contributes disproportionately to political elites, these elites have become more polarized.

These divisions of opinion contribute powerfully to the kind of one-issue politics so characteristic of the present era. Abortion, gun control, gay rights, nuclear energy, affirmative action—all these issues and more make life miserable for the traditional, coalition-seeking politician. Weakened institutions, individualized politics, and the rise of an educated, idea-oriented public combine to make it highly advantageous for political entrepreneurs to identify and mobilize single-issue constituencies and to enlist them, not only into electoral and legislative politics, but into court suits, referendum campaigns, and even calls for constitutional conventions.

To the extent that ideas determine whether the atomized political system will move speedily, sluggishly, or not at all, the principal task of political analysis becomes that of understanding the processes whereby certain ideas become dominant. This requires more subtle techniques for studying public opinion than any that have been routinely employed, techniques that will measure the intensity of feeling as well as its distribution and will distinguish opinions capable of providing the basis for political mobilization from those that are mere expressions of preference. And we require better knowledge about the organizations that shape opinion—the mass and elite media, the universities, and those acronymic groups that manage to devise and disseminate compelling slogans.

In John Fischer's day, scholars studied big business, labor unions, medical societies, and farm groups. When I first studied politics in the 1950s, I learned that there were only six important interest groups: the AFL, the CIO, the American Medical Association, the American Legion, the Chamber of Commerce, and the National Association of Manufacturers. Today, no student could pass a political science exam by giving an answer such as that. Groups have multiplied astronomically; what counts now are ideas more than interests. We need to understand better how elites learn ideas in their colleges and law schools and from the magazines of opinion. How else can we explain, for example, why a generation of legislators who believed in the virtues of business regulation by independent commissions is being replaced by one seeking to deregulate many of those businesses, often over the bitter objections of the regulated industry? Or why a generation that applauded John F. Kennedy's inaugural promise to defend liberty anywhere, at any price, has become one that prefers to minimize risks of every kind, in every place?

We are at a loss for a word or phrase to describe the new features of the political system. Such terms as "veto-group politics" seemed most appropriate for the system that Fischer and later David Riesman described thirty years ago; many discrete facts are summarized in that economical statement. Today, the system is more confused and so our political vocabulary has become more prolix and less precise.

Viewed in a longer historical perspective, what we are seeing may not be all that new. The Congress in which Madison and his immediate successors sat was highly individualized. Strong, institutionalized congressional leadership did not emerge until the latter half of the nineteenth century; one contest for Speaker in 1856 ran to 133 ballots. Factions abounded, but national interest-group organization did not occur until the end of the nineteenth century. "Single-issue" politics existed, the abolition of slavery being the most conspicuous example. But in Madison's time, and for many decades thereafter, national politics was less a career than a hobby; the federal government played a minor role in human affairs; the range of issues with which Congress had to deal was small; and ideological cleavages tended to occur one at a time. Besides, who would stay in Washington during the summer before air conditioning had been invented? Now, governing is a profession, the government plays a large role, and issues tend to pile up, one atop the other, in a network of multiple and profound ideological cleavages. Whether one describes as "fundamental" the changes in institutions and ideas that have accompanied the rise of modern government is in part a matter of style. Yet one must be impressed by the change in the dominant ethos of the times. The period 1890–1920 was the great era of institution building that produced voluntary associations, political parties, corporate enterprises, and congressional leadership, while the last decade or so has been an era that criticized, attacked, and partially dismantled institutions.

From a broader, international perspective, one might say that the changes I have described add up to nothing of fundamental importance. The American constitutional order, with its separate executive and legislative branches and its independent judiciary, remains very different from the British system of cabinet-in-parliament. By the standards of liberals and socialists, the American system remains far more conservative than that of European democracies. Where is our national health insurance, our comprehensive income-maintenance scheme, our government ownership of key industries? By these tests, the American system is conservative. But these broad new policies are now on the horizon and may be enacted soon, albeit many decades after they became part of Western European democracies.

What is striking is that, since the 1930s, there has occurred in this country an extraordinary redistribution of political power without any prior redistribution of income or wealth. Those persons, of the right as well as the left, who are enchanted with economic explanations of political life have their work cut out for them if they insist on ignoring the powerful transformation in ideas that seems to lie at the heart of these changes.

Notes

1. *The New American Political System* (American Enterprise Institute, 1978), 393.
2. See his article, "Imperial Government," in the June 1978 *Commentary*.

2

"Policy Intellectuals" and Public Policy

Originally published in The Public Interest, *Summer 1981*

The "brains trust" of the Franklin Roosevelt administration has grown dramatically into an elaborate set of issue networks inside and outside of government. The 1980 election brought conservative ideas into Washington, just as Johnson's election had brought liberal ones. But the Reagan administration did not manage (or even try very hard) to bring federal policies back to where they had been when Coolidge was president, and the Johnson administration did not complete the more liberal ideas of the New Deal. Today (2010) the Obama administration is trying to do just that, and trying in the teeth of a major recession. It is clear that policy intellectuals have become much more important since this essay was first published.

Not since the 1960s has the course of public policy seemed more under the influence of ideas and so, presumably, of intellectuals. In the 1960s the ideas in question were those of liberal intellectuals and, since liberalism has long been the governing ideology of American polities, the intellectuals then in vogue were brimming with the kind of self-confidence that comes from the belief that they were in the vanguard of an irresistible historical impulse. In the 1980s, the ideas that seemed to influence the administration of President Reagan are about how best to reverse, or at least stem, a political tide that has been running for half a century or more. Not surprisingly, these ideas are more controversial and their proponents feel more embattled than did their predecessors of two decades ago. In the 1960s, the "policy intellectuals" saw themselves as priests of the established order; today, their counterparts think of themselves as missionaries in a hostile country.

19

To find an approximate parallel, one must go back to the early years of the New Deal when the modern American governing system was first put in place. Then, as now, competing ideas struggled for influence; then, as now, there was agreement that an historic turning point had been reached but disagreement over the direction in which to turn. Ellis W. Hawley, in *The New Deal and the Problem of Monopoly*, has provided a vivid account of the conflict among strategies that divided political elites at the time. Some thought the Depression could be ended by ending competition, and their solution was industrial self-government, culminating in the National Industrial Recovery Act. Some thought the solution was national planning, an idea that received the enthusiastic support of intellectuals such as Charles Beard, Rexford Tugwell, John Dewey, and Stuart Chase but the indifference of most policymakers. And still others thought the solution was to reinvigorate competition, by strenuously enforcing the antitrust laws and breaking up large corporations. Though the practitioners of the antitrust approach were mainly lawyers, especially former students of Felix Frankfurter, their practice drew theoretical inspiration from the work of academic economists such as Joan Robinson and Edward Chamblerlain.

Today, the effort to cope with stagflation has led to a conflict involving "supply-siders," who emphasize tax cuts as a way of spurring investment and productivity; fiscal conservatives, who argue for cutting federal expenditures; and monetarists, who stress controlling the money supply. The strength with which each view is held by economists seems inversely proportional to the amount of empirical evidence that it is correct. The practical consequences of adopting one idea or another may well be very great, but economists are deeply divided over what those consequences will be. One of the reasons for that division, as Herbert Stein has noted, is that ultimately economics depends on psychology—that is, on estimates of how people will behave given their perceptions of where the world is heading. About mass psychology we know next to nothing.

The Influence of Intellectuals

Contrary to what their critics often suppose, intellectuals are not usually the authors of particular policies. In no period, perhaps, did intellectuals have greater access to the wielders of political power than they did in the 1960s, and yet scarcely any of the programs enacted then came from their pens or even from their opinions. School administrators pressed for the Elementary and Secondary Education Act; welfare bureaucrats, together with the AFL-CIO, created Medicare and Medicaid; Justice Department lawyers fashioned the federal "war on crime"; congressional staff members and various publicists created many of the environmental and consumer protection laws; agency representatives together with the White House staff devised the War on Poverty; legislators, acting under the prod of an impatient judiciary and a justly aggrieved civil rights movement, wrote the major civil rights laws.

One must be impressed by the extent to which the 1960s, so filled with presidential commissions, task forces, and peripatetic "action intellectuals," produced programs that chiefly reflected the efforts of government bureaucrats and their allied constituencies who had a stake in the management and funding of a proposed policy, working together with the political staffs of legislators and presidents who saw in a new program opportunity for national progress, personal advancement, or both. Intellectuals were asked for their advice and their findings; they gave copiously of the former and sparingly of the latter. But rarely did they actually devise a program or initiate a policy. There may have been two important exceptions to this record of noninfluence: macroeconomic policy, insofar as it was affected by the work of the Council of Economic Advisers and Treasury experts; and military strategy, insofar as it was shaped by "defense intellectuals" in and out of the Pentagon.

If the influence of intellectuals was not to be found in the details of policy, it was nonetheless real, albeit indirect. Intellectuals provided the conceptual language, the ruling paradigms, the empirical examples (note that I say examples, not evidence) that became the accepted assumptions for those in charge of making policy. Intellectuals framed, and to a large degree conducted, the debates about whether this language and these paradigms were correct. The most influential intellectuals were those who managed to link a concept or a theory to the practical needs and ideological predispositions of political activists and government officials. The extent to which this process occurred can be measured by noting the number of occasions on which a government official (or businessman, or interest group leader) was able to preface his remarks with the phrase, "as everyone knows . . ."

It became a widely accepted "fact," for example, that sluggish economic growth would be stimulated, at no serious cost, if the government increased aggregate demand by increasing the federal deficit. Demand could also be increased by cutting taxes, of course, but that had several disadvantages—tax cuts were politically much harder to achieve than spending increases, they opened the door to demands that expenditures be cut, and they implied that individual citizens were better judges of what their money should be spent on than was government.

A somewhat less influential concept was the notion that poverty was essentially the result of a lack of money, and so a rational solution to the problem of poverty was to give more money to persons who had little. This idea, developed by both conservative and liberal economists as well as by intellectual critics of the social service bureaucracy, led to various unsuccessful efforts to move the country toward a negative income tax or a guaranteed annual income (initially disguised, of course, as a "family assistance plan" or "welfare reform"). The advocates of the idea had some powerful images to deploy: a social service strategy involved "meddling bureaucrats" and "endless red tape" as the government tried "to feed the sparrows by feeding the horses." What they did not have was either empirical evidence as to the work-incentive effects of a guaranteed income or persuasive arguments that would reconcile those just above the poverty line to being taxed to help those just below it.

One might multiply such examples endlessly. At one time, "everyone knew" that rehabilitation was the correct perspective through which to view the problem of crime; at a later time, "almost everyone knew" that deterrence was a better perspective. In 1938, when the Civil Aeronautics Act was passed, not a single economist testified against it because "everyone knew" that public regulation was necessary to prevent "ruinous competition" and public subsidy was necessary to help an "infant industry." Exactly forty years later, no economist could be found to testify in favor of airline regulation because by then everyone knew that competition was a more efficient way of controlling prices and routes. For about a quarter of a century, historians and others drew one lesson from the experience of Munich and Pearl Harbor: unchecked aggression breeds further aggression. After Vietnam, the lesson was changed: efforts to check aggression will breed further aggression, which in any event is not aggression at all, but "national liberation."

The most important source of intellectual influence on public policy, however, arises not out of the way in which particular problems are defined, but out of the definition of what constitutes a problem and what standards ought to be used in judging its problematic character. The two most powerful and enduring ideas in American political culture are so deeply shared that we are unaware of how pervasive they are—except, perhaps, when we visit other nations that have been shaped by quite different ideas. One idea draws on that part of our Puritan heritage that attached a high value to the rationalization and moralization of society. The other draws on a tradition that, though still ancient, is about two centuries younger than the first: the theory of natural rights, defined in 1776 as the right to life, liberty, and property and expressed today as a desire to maximize individual self-expression and the claims that the individual may make against society.

A nation that had been formed out of a feudal aristocracy or by the slow extraction of concessions from a divinely inspired ruler would not have these intellectual traditions. It would instead have a political culture that retained some substantial measure of agreement that citizens had obligations to the state and ought to defer to its officials. The relations between the state and the church would have been controversial, but the state would not have taken, in the name of freedom of conscience, the view that the church (or the churches) did not exist or that religion had no place in civil affairs. Such a society would have had relatively few voluntary associations and neighborhood groups bent on improving the quality of life at the local level; by the same token, such a society would have erected far fewer barriers to police and court action designed to protect public safety in those neighborhoods. A state with a more collectivist origin and less imbued with the philosophy of individual rights would have been quicker than ours to adopt certain social welfare measures; a state without a Puritan compulsion to perfect man would have been slower than ours to enact laws to fix up the environment and regulate business-consumer relations.

Obviously, these two intellectual and cultural traditions are partially in conflict. The more we extend the scope of rights, the harder it is to regulate and to improve; the more regulation, the narrower the scope of rights. As individuals, we sometimes try to reconcile the two by insisting on the maximum array of rights with respect to matters of self-expression or private conduct and relegating our desire to rationalize society to the domain of corporations (which need regulation) and the underprivileged (who require uplifting). But such a categorization will not work, as we discover when we try to decide about rent control, or the regulation of corporate advertising, or busing to achieve racial integration, or quotas for the admission of students to universities.

Rather than searching American history for some device by which the philosophy of rights and the desire to moralize can be brought into some Grand Synthesis, it is better to view that history as alternating periods in which one and then the other impulse becomes dominant. The Puritan desire for the cooperative commonwealth and the moralizing community reappears in the settlement house movement of the turn of the century, the anticompetitive "business association" movement of the 1920s, the continuing desire to find a formula by which criminals may be rehabilitated, and the endless hopes we entertain for education. The revolutionary appeal of a philosophy of individual rights animated the antislavery movement of the 1830s, the feminist movement that began at almost the same time, the desire to find in the Constitution a "right of privacy," the periodic efforts to deal with the mentally ill and the criminal by deinstitutionalizing them, and the tendency to decriminalize more and more behaviors.

At any given moment in history, an influential idea, and thus an influential intellectual, is one that provides a persuasive simplification of some policy question that is consistent with the particular mix of core values then held by the political elite. "Regulation" and "deregulation" have been such ideas; so also have "balanced budgets" versus "compensatory fiscal policy" and "integration" versus "affirmative action." Clarifying and making persuasive those ideas is largely a matter of argument and the careful use of analogies; rarely (the exceptions will be discussed below) does this process involve matters of proof and evidence of the sort that is, in their scholarly as opposed to their public lives, supposed to be the particular skill and obligation of intellectuals in the university.

Doing Intellectual Work

There is little wrong with intellectuals taking part, along with everyone else, in the process by which issues are defined, assumptions altered, and language supplied. But some of them, particularly university scholars, are supposed to participate under a special obligation—namely, to make clear what they know as opposed to what they wish. Those who listen to them ought to understand the circumstances under which intellectuals are more or less likely to know what they claim to know. Not all intellectuals are scholars— that is, persons producing and testing ideas under rules governing the quality of evidence—but those who are generally acknowledge, if they do not always follow, the thrust of those rules. Let us consider some examples of intellectuals doing their work poorly or well.

I start with three examples of scholarly work either poorly done or badly used. The Phillips curve, formulated in the late 1950s, purported to show that for about a century there was a trade-off between inflation and unemployment: when unemployment was high, wages or prices were falling; when unemployment was low, prices were rising. There was no evidence that one thing caused the other and, as several economists were later to show, good reason to believe that one did not cause the other except in the very short run. Moreover, even the apparent correlation between unemployment and inflation was adduced from a period, much of it in the nineteenth century, when long-term declines in prices and wages were still possible. But as Allan H. Meltzer was later to write, despite the difficulties with the theory, "Phillips curves jumped quickly from the scholarly journals to the Executive Office of the President." The theory retained its grip on the minds of many economists and even more policymakers for the better part of two decades. Policies enacted in its name served to increase inflation without decreasing unemployment.

The doctrine of mutual assured destruction (MAD) is an exquisitely complex exercise in strategic logic based on a quite simple premise: one nation will not attack another if it knows in advance that it will be destroyed by its victim's retaliatory capacity. As it evolved among American defense intellectuals and military planners, it required that both the United States and the Soviet Union make their cities hostage to one another's atomic weapons. MAD was based on a number of assumptions: That the United States would have the political will to retaliate, promptly and with nuclear weapons, if attacked by the Soviet Union. That neither side would think it had anything to gain by building a nuclear strike force greater than that necessary to destroy some large percentage of the other side's civilian population. That neither side would try to protect its cities against missile attack (if they were protected, they could not be hostages). That neither side would think it possible to win a nuclear exchange.

It is not clear that these assumptions are still plausible, if indeed they ever were. Though we cannot know with certainty the intentions of the USSR, their missile building program is consistent with the view that there is a military and political advantage to be had from possessing a larger nuclear force, that a nuclear exchange may be winnable, and that defending their cities from nuclear attack, passively (with civil defense) or actively (with missiles), is worthwhile.

For many years, though less so today than formerly, it was widely believed among intellectuals that the proper solution to America's heroin problem involved some form of decriminalization. If addicts can get heroin cheaply and legally, they will have no incentive to steal. If they have no such incentives, the crime rate will fall dramatically. England, it was thought, had adopted just such a system and as a result it had relatively few addicts and little crime. There is some truth in this argument (as there is in the others I have criticized) but not the whole truth. There is a good deal of evidence that heroin consumption, and thus heroin addiction, increases as the price of heroin, or the difficulty of finding it, decreases. Thus decriminalizing heroin in an effort to reduce crime among confirmed addicts will have the effect of increasing the number of addicts, probably by a very large number. The number of known addicts in England increased dramatically when heroin was easily available; what is known today as the English system was the result of an effort to reduce the drug's availability by placing it under tighter government control. There are important disputes about some of the facts (how many addicts steal because they are addicts, how elastic the demand for heroin may be), but the essential issue is not a factual one at all. It is rather a moral and political one—how much of an increase in the number of addicts will you tolerate for a given decrease in the amount of crime by addicts? As conventionally set out in intellectual discussions, that question is usually skirted in favor of the confident assertion that there are no important trade-offs.

Now let me offer three examples of intellectual work well done. For decades, economists have attempted to estimate the effects on consumer welfare of government regulation of prices and government restrictions on entry in a variety of industries. The Brookings Institution sponsored a series of studies on regulation, and shortly thereafter the American Enterprise Institute launched its own series. The research dealt with aviation, railroads, trucking, shipping, electric utilities, securities exchanges, natural gas, oil, milk, and banking; and certain industries, notably aviation, were analyzed by several different scholars (Richard E. Caves, George C. Eads, James C. Miller III, William A. Jordan) located at different academic institutions and having, I think, a variety of political views. The simplest summary of this work has become well known: price and entry regulation in these industries has raised costs to the consumer above what they would have been had prices and entry been determined by market competition.

The effects on educational attainment of observable differences among schools has been a matter of almost continuous inquiry since the publication, in 1966, of the report by James S. Coleman and his colleagues. The original findings of the Coleman Report, put baldly, were that differences in the readily measureable features of schools—expenditures, pupil-teacher ratios, building quality, and the like—had little or no effect on academic achievement once you controlled for the family background of the pupils, and this was true for both whites and blacks. The original Coleman data were subject to the most intensive reanalysis by a variety of scholars, including Christopher Jencks, David Armor, David Cohen, and many others. New studies were undertaken, here and abroad. Though some quibbles arose, the central findings of the Coleman Report remained intact. Scholars then began to ask whether certain hard-to-measure, intangible aspects of schooling might make a difference—a not unreasonable possibility, given the enormous efforts made by parents to ensure that their children attended "good schools," efforts that obviously assumed there was such a thing as a good school. Gradually it became clear that how the teacher conducted his or her classes and how the principal managed his or her teachers might well make a very great difference independent of curricula, physical facilities, teacher education, or pupil-teacher ratios. There is evidence to this effect from Eric A. Hanushek, who summarized the findings for American schools, from Michael Rutter, who looked at London schoolchildren, and from Thomas Sowell, who wanted to understand why certain all-black high schools were so much more successful than others. In sum, we are beginning to develop a clearer understanding of what aspects of schooling make a difference, and how great a difference;

unfortunately, we are at the same time learning that those things that make a difference are hardest to measure or to manipulate.

For the better part of two centuries, the most progressive elements in society held tenaciously to the view that the proper social response to crime was to attempt the rehabilitation of the criminal and that other objectives—deterrence, incapacitation, retribution—were misguided, immoral, or likely to make matters worse. Beginning in the 1940s and extending over several decades, a number of scholars here and abroad sought to discover whether criminals could be rehabilitated, by plan and in large numbers. The investigations strongly suggested that most rehabilitative efforts failed, that the better the evaluation of the effort the less likely the effort would prove a success, and that the attempt to make rehabilitation the goal often resulted in unfair or inequitable penalties being imposed on offenders. When Robert Martinson published in 1974 his summary of over two hundred such studies, a fresh attempt was made to assess the literature. A panel of the National Academy of Sciences reexamined a sample of the studies and found that Martinson's discouraging conclusion was essentially correct, though the panel left open the possibility that some desirable rehabilitative effects might emerge from some properly designed projects. And there exist bits and pieces of evidence that rehabilitation may work for certain kinds of offenders under certain circumstances.

By now the reader may be entertaining the suspicion that I have somehow arranged for the examples of defective intellectual work to be those that reach conclusions of which I do not approve and for the examples of successful intellectual work to be ones that reach conclusions of which I do approve. Needless to say, I think my summary is fair and nonpartisan, but for the skeptics let me add one additional example in which research tending to support a policy view I like has not yet reached a level of clarity and consistency that would lead me to conclude that the matter is settled.

A number of efforts have been made to determine whether an increase in the probability of going to prison for a given offense will, other things being equal, be associated with a lower rate of committing that offense. A large number of studies have found that as imprisonment probabilities go down, crime rates go up. The work of Isaac Ehrlich is perhaps the best known of these studies, but there are many others. It turns out, however, that there are a large number of methodological difficulties that prevent one from concluding, without reservation, that the increase in imprisonment rates causes a decrease in crime rates. These difficulties chiefly arise from the fact that most of the studies use data of uneven quality and rely on aggregating those data into very large units (counties, states, or nations), that are then compared. A panel of the National Academy of Sciences (of which I was a member) identified a number of problems with such studies and concluded, cautiously, that the "evidence certainly favors a proposition supporting deterrence more than it favors one asserting that deterrence is absent, [but] even though criminal sanctions surely influence at least some criminal behavior, the data from these aggregate studies do not yet conclusively establish a deterrent effect." Personally, I would be less cautious than the panel, for studies of the behavior of individuals and of business firms facing differing court sanctions—studies not subject to some of the problems discussed by the panel—are strongly consistent with the deterrence hypothesis. But I would certainly agree with the panel that, however one evaluates existing studies, one is not yet in a position to predict what would happen to crime if a city or state made a particular change in its criminal justice system.

Why Some Intellectual Products Are Better

Not every reader will agree with my examples of good and bad policy-related intellectual work, even after I have added a pet idea of mine to the not-yet-very-good category. Such persons are invited to substitute their own examples. My argument is that after inspecting any reasonable list of good or not-so-good intellectual efforts we will be able to make some generalizations about the characteristics of better or worse policy analysis.

The better examples tend to have these features: They involve statements about what has happened in the past, not speculations about what may happen in the future. They are evaluations of policies that have already been implemented. Because some firms are regulated, for example, we can compare the distribution of costs and benefits of that regulation before and after the policy was implemented. If any single fact has been crucially significant in showing that price and entry regulation have adverse effects on consumers, it is the comparison of rates charged by unregulated intrastate airlines (for example, those linking San Francisco and Los Angeles) with those charged by regulated interstate airlines (for example, those connecting Boston and Washington, D.C.). Even so, it is necessary to look carefully for other factors besides regulation that might have affected prices (there were some, but they were not decisive).

Similarly, conclusions about the effect of rehabilitation programs on offenders were most persuasive when they derived from measuring, not the criminal tendencies of persons who in the ordinary course of events might or might not have received some form of treatment, but the actual effect of a particular program on a random sample of persons compared to the effect of doing nothing to an equivalent random sample of offenders. Much of the debate about the original Coleman Report on schooling arose from the fact that it analyzed the natural variation in educational attainment among persons in existing schools. The most impressive support for its central findings (and for some interesting new findings about how schools may make a difference) came from following a specific group of youngsters as they worked their way through a dozen or so schools of differing quality (as was done by Rutter in London).

The intellectual claims on behalf of the Phillips curve, by contrast, were based on projections into contemporary America of observed relationships between employment and inflation in past eras and other places. The claims about British heroin policy were based on a misunderstanding of that policy extrapolated to a wholly different culture and with little regard to the full range of costs and benefits of even the original British policy. The arguments in favor of MAD made assumptions about the likely motives of our adversaries that were not susceptible to empirical verification, and were probably wrong, at least in the long run.

Almost any form of policy prescription involves reasoning by analogy: If two phenomena are alike in one respect, they will be alike in another respect. If something works in one circumstance, it will also work in another similar circumstance. The case for analogical reasoning is stronger where there are more similarities between two situations, but it can rarely, if ever, be conclusive. Two situations may be different in some important but unsuspected feature. The closest we may come to making a conclusive argument is when the research involves the evaluation of a controlled experiment; the next closest involves the evaluation of a quasi-experiment supplied by historical circumstance. The best studies of criminal rehabilitation were based on controlled experiments; the best case against airline regulation was based on the quasi-experiment created by the existence of unregulated intrastate airlines in California.

Beyond the method employed, the quality of an intellectual argument about the likely effects of a policy is highest when there have been many cases studied by many different investigators, using different sources of data. If they agree, it does not prove they are right (their agreement may depend on an unexamined false assumption they all share), but it increases the odds they are right. The surgeon general of the United States was able to draw upon hundreds, perhaps thousands, of studies of the effect of smoking on health in reaching his conclusions; by contrast, as Lawrence Sherman has pointed out, our knowledge of the effect of the police on violent crime must depend on either the judgment of practitioners or the results of one or two studies.

The Role of Intellectuals

If my argument is correct, then the role for intellectuals as *scholars* (rather than as partisan advocates or insightful citizens) in the making of public policy is likely to be small. There are relatively few areas of public dispute wherein one can find the amassed data, the careful analyses, and the evaluated experiments that would entitle us to assign a very large weight to scholarly arguments about the likely effect of doing one thing rather than another. Moreover, for scholars to know anything at all about what works, it is often necessary for the government to try a new policy under circumstances that permit independent observers to find out what happens. This does not often happen, but it happens occasionally, as when the government tried to find out the consequences of providing persons with a guaranteed annual income. But even when it happens, it is risky to assume that a small-scale experiment among persons who know they are the objects of an experiment (and who know that someday soon the experiment will end) will produce the same results as a permanent national program.

It would be interesting to know, for example, if the much-discussed Laffer curve accurately shows the relationship between tax rates and tax revenues. At present, there is not more evidence for it than there once was for the Phillips curve. And such evidence as does exist is highly analogical:

circumstances here and now must be sufficiently like circumstances elsewhere and in the past so that a sharp reduction in tax rates now will have the same effect as they may have had twenty years ago in this country or more recently in other countries. We are not likely to find out unless we try, but unfortunately we cannot try in incremental or experimental steps: we either do it decisively, and for a long term, or not at all. Under these circumstances, it is a bold scholar indeed who will speak confidently about what will happen.

All this suggests that intellectuals are probably at their best—that is, do things they are best suited to do—when they tell people in power that something they tried did not work as they expected. No one should be surprised, then, if scholars who behave in their traditional roles turn out to be highly unpopular.

Congress seems bent on preserving the fiction that scholarship can and should operate by identifying problems, amassing evidence, and then devising solutions. If scholars have not done this, then it must be their fault, and they should be ignored. But the study of human affairs can rarely proceed in this manner. Good intellectual work is typically retrospective rather than prospective, and even then its findings are ordinarily highly dependent on the particular circumstances of time, place, and culture. Moreover, it is quite difficult, if not impossible, to predict in advance which scholarly proposal will produce truly interesting results. None of these difficulties can be overcome by demands from Congress that research be more "applied" or that greater external control be exerted over the research that is done.

Scholars need no additional urging to attend to areas of national interest: they already rush like lemmings in directions set by policy. Research on the consequences of schooling, desegregation, government regulation, and crime control methods followed the emergence of public concern about such matters. The contribution such research can make is to establish and sustain among a large number of practitioners a continuing intellectual dialogue by which assumptions are questioned, early findings reexamined, and new avenues of inquiry identified. Knowledge may or may not accumulate, but the standards of evidence are clarified and bad ideas are (usually) detected. Moreover, out of this sifting, new ways of thinking sometimes arise. This last may be the most important result of all.

Intellectuals do not simply test, evaluate, or (where bold) predict. They supply, as I remarked at the outset, the concepts by which we define important parts of reality. They lead us to see old relationships in new ways. They do this without drawing on any special training or expertise, and their conceptual language is rarely susceptible to verification; in short, what a natural scientist or social scientist learns in preparing himself to be an intellectual is rarely what gives him that influence that some intellectuals have.

There are countless examples of an idea serving, quickly or gradually, to alter the terms of a debate and realign existing political coalitions. When Milton Friedman first proposed over two decades ago that parents be given vouchers to purchase education for their children from any of several competing purveyors, the idea was either ignored or derided. Once, in about 1960, I tried to convince a group of school officials of the merit of the idea. I recall one of them referring to me as a "communist." Today the voucher idea, though not universally accepted, is taken seriously as a way of altering the production and consumption of education. The tuition tax credit, should it be adopted, may be a way station en route to the voucher. We still do not know whether it is a workable, or even a sound, idea, but we do know that one cannot seriously discuss public education without considering it.

Criminal deterrence is another such idea. I think it a plausible one, though I cannot prove its validity to skeptics. But the willingness of intellectuals today, as opposed to those ten years ago, to take the idea seriously and weigh it against other goals of criminal justice has altered, at least for the time being, the terms in which crime is discussed.

So also with supply-side economics. What is most striking about this theory is not the weight of evidence and argumentation mustered on its behalf, but the fact that in the space of a few short years it has fundamentally altered the terms of debate about economic policy. Not too long ago it was still possible, albeit only with some major simplification, to explain to students that macroeconomic policy was either Keynesian or monetarist. Now there is a third (and possibly a fourth or fifth) contender. Political conservatives, who once knew only that they disliked that feature of Keynesian economics that led to rising government expenditures, now discover that they must choose between several competing remedies for this problem: cutting taxes (and cutting expenditures on the side, at least a little bit) or cutting expenditures (and maybe leaving taxes where they are), or possibly controlling the money supply and forgetting about the budget.

In short, what intellectuals chiefly bring to policy debates, and what chiefly accounts for their influence, is not knowledge but theory. Someone once jokingly referred to a well-known West Coast think tank as "the leisure of the theory class"; the phrase was mistaken only in implying that theorizing and leisure are compatible activities. We have seen one particular kind of theory—the motion of economic man, rationally pursuing his self-interest—make great headway in some quarters only to be met by other theories moving in a different direction. There is little point in denouncing theory as an inadequate substitute for experience, knowledge, or prudence (which it is); it will be propounded, it will affect policy, and those skilled at formulating it will rise in influence. Moreover, theorizing is not the same as empty talk. Good theory calls attention to obvious truths that were previously overlooked, finds crucial flaws in existing theories, and reinterprets solid evidence in a new light. And some theories, if adopted, will make us all better off. The problem is to know which ones.

3

The Rediscovery of Character: Private Virtue and Public Policy

Originally published in The Public Interest, Fall 1985

This essay, written to help celebrate the twentieth anniversary of The Public Interest, *tried to draw attention to an increased concern with human character on the part of the public and to a lesser extent the government. In later years, this concern led to the passage of two laws: a welfare reform law (during the Clinton administration) and a law that emphasized student achievement (during the George W. Bush administration). The growth of charter schools and educational voucher programs, all generated by state and private activity, is exceptional testimony to this preoccupation with character.*

The most important change in how one defines the public interest that I have witnessed over the last twenty years has been a deepening concern for the development of character in the citizenry. An obvious indication of this shift has been the increased prominence of such social issues as abortion and school prayer. A less obvious but I think more important change has been the growing awareness that a variety of public problems can be understood, and perhaps addressed, only if they are seen as arising out of a defect in character formation.

The Public Interest began publication at about the time that economics was becoming the preferred mode of policy analysis. Its very first issue (1965) contained an article by Daniel Patrick Moynihan hailing the triumph of macroeconomics: "Men are learning how to make an industrial economy work" as evidenced by the impressive ability of economists not only to predict economic events accurately but to control them by, for example, delivering on the promise of full employment. The early issues of the magazine are filled with economic analyses: the suggestion that poverty be dealt with by direct income transfers in the form of a negative income tax or family allowances; James Tobin's full-scale proposal for a negative income tax; articles by Virginia Held and William Gorham arguing that program planning and budgeting would rationalize the allocative decisions of the federal government; Thomas C. Schelling's economic analysis of organized crime; Christopher Jencks's call for a school voucher system; and an article by Gordon Tulluck arguing that crime increases when rational individuals see an increase in the net benefit of criminality.

To be sure, there were criticisms of some of these views. Alvin L. Schorr, James C. Vadakian, and Nathan Glazer published essays attacking aspects of the negative income tax, and Aaron Wildavsky expressed his skepticism about program budgeting. But the criticisms themselves often accepted the economic assumptions of those being criticized. Schorr, for example, argued that the negative income tax was unworkable because it did not resolve the conflict between a strong work incentive and an adequate payment to the needy. Schorr proposed instead a system of children's allowances and improved social security coverage, but he did not dissent from the view that the only thing wrong with poor people was that they did not have enough money and the conviction that they had a "right" to enough. Tobin was quick to point out that he and Schorr were on the same side, differing only in minor details.

A central assumption of economics is that "tastes" (which include what noneconomists would call values and beliefs, as well as interests) can be taken as given and are not problematic. All that is interesting in human behavior is how it changes in response to changes in the costs and benefits of alternative courses of action. All that is necessary in public policy is to arrange the incentives confronting voters, citizens, firms, bureaucrats, and politicians so that they will behave in a socially optimal way. An optimal policy involves efficient allocation—purchasing the greatest amount of some good for a given cost, or minimizing the cost of a given amount of some good.

This view so accords with common sense in countless aspects of ordinary life that, for many purposes, its value is beyond dispute. Moreover, enough political decisions are manifestly so inefficient or rely so excessively on issuing commands (instead of arranging incentives) that very little harm and much good can be done by urging public officials to "think economically" about public policy. But over the last two decades, this nation has come face to face with problems that do not seem to respond, or to respond enough, to changes in incentives. They do not respond, it seems, because the people whose behavior we wish to change do not have the right "tastes" or discount the future too heavily. To put it plainly, they lack character. I illustrate this point by considering four areas of public policy: schooling, welfare, public finance, and crime.

Schooling

Nothing better illustrates the changes in how we think about policy than the problem of poor educational attainment and student conduct. As every expert on schooling knows, the massive survey by James Coleman of public schools found that differences in the objective inputs to such schools—pupil-teacher ratios, the number of books in the library, per-pupil expenditures, the age and quality of buildings—had no independent effect on student achievement as measured by standardized tests of verbal ability.

But as many scholars have forgotten, the Coleman Report also found that educational achievement was profoundly affected by the family background and peer-group environment of the pupil. And those who did notice this finding understandably despaired of devising a program that would improve the child's family background or social environment. Soon, many specialists had concluded that schools could make no difference in a child's life prospects, and so the burden of enhancing those prospects would have to fall on other measures. (To Christopher Jencks, the inability of the schools to reduce social inequality was an argument for socialism.)

Parents, of course, acted as if the Coleman Report had never been written. They sought, often at great expense, communities that had good schools, never doubting for a moment that they could tell the difference between good ones and bad ones or that this difference in school quality would make a difference in their child's education. The search for good schools in the face of evidence that there was no objective basis for that search seemed paradoxical, even irrational.

In 1979, however, Michael Rutter and his colleagues in England published a study that provided support for parental intuition by building on the neglected insights of the Coleman Report. In *Fifteen Thousand Hours*, the Rutter group reported what they had learned from following a large number of children from a working-class section of inner London as they moved through a dozen nonselective schools in their community. Like Coleman before him, Rutter found that the objective features of the schools made little difference; like almost every other scholar, he found that verbal intelligence at age ten was the best single predictor of educational attainment in the high school years. But unlike Coleman, he looked at differences in that attainment across schools, holding individual ability constant. Rutter found that the schools in inner London had very different effects on their pupils, not only in educational achievement but also in attendance, classroom behavior, and even delinquency. Some schools did a better job than others in teaching children and managing their behavior.

The more effective schools had two distinctive characteristics. First, they had a more balanced mix of children—that is, they contained a substantial number of children of at least average intellectual ability. By contrast, schools that were less effective had a disproportionate number of low-ability students. If you are a pupil of below-average ability, you do better, both academically and behaviorally, if you attend a school with a large number of students who are somewhat abler than you. The intellectual abilities of the students, it turned out, were far more important than their ethnic or class characteristics in producing this desirable balance.

Second, the more effective schools had a distinctive ethos: an emphasis on academic achievement, the regular assignment of homework, the consistent and fair use of rewards (especially praise) to enforce agreed-upon standards of conduct, and energetic teacher involvement in directing classroom work. Subsequent research by others has generally confirmed the Rutter account, so much so that educational specialists are increasingly discussing what has come to be known as the "effective schools" model.

What is striking about the desirable school ethos is that it so obviously resembles what almost every developmental psychologist describes as the desirable family ethos. Parents who are warm and caring but who also use discipline in a fair and consistent manner are those parents who, other things being equal, are least likely to produce delinquent offspring. A decent family is one that instills a decent character in its children; a good school is one that takes up and continues in a constructive manner this development of character.

Teaching students with the right mix of abilities in a classroom with the appropriate ethos may be easier in private than in public schools. This fact helps explain why Coleman (joined now by Thomas Hoffer and Sally Kilgore) was able to suggest in the 1982 book, *High School Achievement*, that private and parochial high schools may do somewhat better than public ones in improving the vocabulary and mathematical skills of students, and that this private-school advantage may be largely the result of the better behavior of children in those classrooms. In the authors' words, "achievement and discipline are intimately intertwined." Public schools that combine academic demands and high disciplinary standards produce greater educational achievement than public schools that do not. As it turns out, private and parochial schools are better able to sustain these desirable habits of work behavior—this greater display of good character—than are public ones.

Welfare

Another famous document appeared at about the same time as the Coleman Report: the Moynihan Report on the problems of the black family (officially, the U.S. Department of Labor document entitled *The Negro Family: The Case for National Action*). The storm of controversy that report elicited is well known. Despite Moynihan's efforts to keep the issue alive by publishing several essays on the welfare problem in America, the entire subject of single-parent families in particular and black families in general became an occasion for the exchange of mutual recriminations instead of a topic of scientific inquiry and policy entrepreneurship. Serious scholarly work, if it existed at all, was driven underground, and policymakers were at pains to avoid the matter except, occasionally, under the guise of "welfare reform," which meant (if you were a liberal) raising the level of benefits or (if you were a conservative) cutting them. By the end of the 1960s, almost everybody in Washington had in this sense become a conservative; welfare reform, as Moynihan remarked, was dead.

Twenty years after the Moynihan Report, Moynihan himself could deliver at Harvard a lecture in which he repeated the observations he had made in 1965, but this time to an enthusiastic audience and widespread praise in the liberal media. At the same time, Glenn C. Loury, a black economist, could publish an essay in which he observed that almost everything Moynihan had said in 1965 had proved true—except that Moynihan did not predict that today, single-parent families would be twice as common as when he first called the matter to public attention. The very title of Loury's essay suggested how times had changed: whereas leaders once spoke of "welfare reform" as if the problem was to find the most cost-effective way to distribute aid to needy families, Loury was now prepared to speak of "The Moral Quandary of the Black Community."

Two decades that could have been devoted to thought and experimentation had been frittered away. We are no closer today than we were in 1965 to understanding why black children are usually raised by one parent rather than by two. To the extent the matter was addressed at all, it was usually done by assuming that welfare payments provided an incentive for families to dissolve. To deal with this, some people embraced the negative income tax (or as President Nixon rechristened it, the Family Assistance Plan) because it would provide benefits to all poor families, broken or not, and thus remove incentive for dissolution.

There were good reasons to be somewhat skeptical of that view. If the system of payments under the Aid to Families with Dependent Children (AFDC) program was to blame for the rise in single-parent families, why did the rise occur so dramatically among blacks but not to nearly the same extent among whites? If AFDC provided an incentive for men to beget children without assuming responsibility for supporting them, why was the illegitimacy rate rising even in states that did not require the father to be absent from the home for the family to obtain assistance? If AFDC created so perverse a set of incentives, why did these incentives have so large an effect in the 1960s and 1970s (when single-parent families were increasing by leaps and bounds) and so little, if any, effect in the 1940s and 1950s (when such families scarcely increased at all)? And if AFDC were the culprit, how is it that poor, single-parent families rose in number during a decade (the 1970s) when the value of AFDC benefits in real dollars was declining?

Behavior does change with changes in incentives. The results of the negative income tax experiments certainly show that. In the Seattle and Denver experiments, the rate of family dissolution was much higher among families who received the guaranteed annual income than among similar families who did not—36 percent higher in the case of whites, 42 percent higher in the case of blacks. Men getting the cash benefits reduced their hours of work by 9 percent, women by 20 percent, and young males without families by 43 percent.

Charles Murray, whose 1984 book, *Losing Ground*, has done so much to focus attention on the problem of welfare, generally endorses the economic explanation for the decline of two-parent families. The evidence from the negative income tax experiments is certainly consistent with his view, and he makes a good case that the liberalization of welfare eligibility rules in the 1960s contributed to the sudden increase in the AFDC caseload. But as he is the first to admit, we lack the data to fully explain the rise of single-parent families; the best he can do is to offer a mental experiment showing how young, poor men and women might rationally respond to the alternative benefits of work for a two-parent family and welfare payments for a one-parent family. He rejects the notion that character, the Zeitgeist, or cultural differences are necessary to an explanation. But he cannot show that young, poor men and women in fact responded to AFDC as he assumes they did, nor can he explain the racial differences in rates or the rise in caseloads at a time of declining benefits. He notes an alternative explanation that cannot be ruled out: during the 1960s, a large number of persons who once thought of being on welfare as a temporary and rather embarrassing expedient came to regard it as a right that they would not be deterred from exercising. The result of that change can be measured: whereas in 1967, 63 percent of the persons eligible for AFDC were on the rolls, by 1970 91 percent were.

In short, the character of a significant number of persons changed. To the extent one thinks that change was fundamentally wrong, then, as Loury has put it, the change creates a moral problem. What does one do about such a moral problem? Lawrence Mead has suggested invigorating the work requirement associated with welfare, so that anyone exercising a "right" to welfare will come to understand that there is a corresponding obligation. Murray has proposed altering the incentives by increasing the difficulty of getting welfare, or the shame of having it, so as to provide positive rewards for not having children, at least out of wedlock. But nobody has yet come to grips with how one might test a way of using either obligations or incentives to alter character so that people who once thought it acceptable to produce illegitimate children will now think it wrong.

Public Finance

We have a vast and rising governmental deficit. Amidst the debate about how one might best reduce that deficit (or more typically, reduce the rate of increase in it), scarcely anyone asks why we have not always had huge deficits.

If you believe that voters and politicians seek rationally to maximize their self-interest, then you would expect most people to transfer wealth from future generations to present ones. If you want the federal government to provide you with some benefit and you cannot persuade other voters to pay for your benefit with higher taxes, then you should be willing to have the government borrow to pay for that benefit. Since every voter has something he would like from the government, each has an incentive to obtain that benefit with funds to be repaid by future generations.

There are, of course, some constraints on unlimited debt financing. Accumulated debt charges from past generations must be financed by this generation, and if these charges are heavy there may well develop some apprehension about adding to them. If some units of government default on their loans, there are immediate economic consequences. But these constraints are not strong enough to inhibit more than marginally the rational desire to let one's grandchildren pay (in inflation-devalued dollars) the cost of present indulgences.

That being so, why is it that large deficits, except in wartime, have been a feature of public finance only in the past few decades? What kept voters and politicians from buying on credit heavily and continuously beginning with the first days of the republic?

James M. Buchanan, in his 1984 presidential address to the Western Economic Association, has offered one explanation for this paradox. He has suggested that public finance was once subject to a moral constraint—namely, the belief that it was right to pay as you go and accumulate capital, and wrong to borrow heavily and squander capital. Max Weber, of course, argued that essential to the rise of capitalism was a widely shared belief (he ascribed it to Protestantism) in the moral propriety of deferring present consumption in order to acquire future benefits. Buchanan has recast this somewhat: he argues that a Victorian morality inhibited Anglo-American democracies from giving in to their selfish desire to beggar their children.

Viewed in light of this explanation, John Maynard Keynes was not simply an important economist, he was a moral revolutionary. He subjected to rational analysis the conventional restraints on deficit financing, not in order to show that debt was always good but to prove that it was not necessarily bad. Deficit financing should be judged, he argued, by its practical effect, not by its moral quality.

Buchanan is a free-market economist, and thus a member of a group not ordinarily given to explaining behavior in any terms other than the pursuit of self-interest narrowly defined. This fact makes all the more significant his argument that economic analysts must understand "how morals impact on choice, and especially how an erosion of moral precepts can modify the established functioning of economic and political institutions."

A rejoinder can be made to the Buchanan explanation of deficit financing. Much of the accumulated debt is a legacy of having fought wars, a legacy that can be justified on both rational and moral grounds (who wishes to lose a war, or to leave for one's children a Europe dominated by Hitler?). Another part of the debt exists because leaders miscalculated the true costs of desirable programs. According to projections made in 1965, Medicare was supposed to cost less than $9 billion a year in 1990; in 1985, the bill was already running in excess of $70 billion a year. Military pensions seemed appropriate when men were being called to service; only in retrospect is their total cost appreciated. The Reagan tax cuts were not designed to impose heavy debts on our children but to stimulate investment and economic growth; only later did it become obvious that they have contributed far more to the deficit than to economic growth. The various subsidies given to special-interest groups seemed like a small price to pay for insuring the support of a heterogeneous people for a distant government; no one could have foreseen their cumulative burden.

No doubt there is some truth in the proposition that our current level of debt is the result of miscalculation and good intentions gone awry. But what strengthens Buchanan's argument, I believe, is the direction of these miscalculations (if that is what they were) and the nature of these good intentions. In almost every instance, leaders proposing a new policy erred in the direction of understating rather than overstating future costs; in almost every instance, evidence of a good intention was taken to be government action rather than inaction. Whether one wishes to call it a shift in moral values or not, one must be struck by the systematic and consistent bias in how we debated public programs beginning in the 1930s but especially evident in the 1960s. It is hard to remember it now, but there once was a time, lasting from 1789 to well into the 1950s, when the debate over almost any new proposal was about whether it was legitimate for the government to do this at all. These were certainly the terms in which Social Security, civil rights, Medicare, and government regulation of business were first addressed. By the 1960s, the debate was much different: how much should we spend (not, should we spend anything at all); how can a policy be made cost-effective (not, should we have such a policy in the first place). The character of public discourse changed and, I suspect, in ways that suggest a change in the nature of public character.

Crime

I have written more about crime than any other policy issue, and so my remarks on our changing understanding of this problem are to a large degree remarks about changes in my own way of thinking about it. Nowhere have the methods of economics and policy analysis had greater or more salutary effect than in scholarly discussions of criminal justice. For purposes of designing public policies, it has proved useful to think of would-be offenders as mostly young males who compare the net benefits of crime with those of work and leisure. Such thinking, and the rather considerable body of evidence that supports it, leads us to expect that changes in the net benefits of crime affect the level of crime in society. To the extent that policymakers and criminologists have become less hostile to the idea of altering behavior by altering its consequences, progress has been made. Even if the amount by which crime is reduced by these measures is modest (as I think in a free society it will be), the pursuit of these policies conforms more fully than does the rehabilitative idea to our concept of justice—namely, that each person should receive his due.

But long-term changes in crime rates exceed anything that can be explained by either rational calculation or the varying proportion of young males in the population. Very little in either contemporary economics or conventional criminology equips us to understand the decline in reported crime rates during the second half of the nineteenth century and the first part of the twentieth despite rapid industrialization and urbanization, a large influx of poor immigrants, the growing ethnic heterogeneity of society, and widening class cleavages. Very little in the customary language of policy analysis helps us explain why Japan should have such abnormally low crime rates despite high population densities, a history that glorifies samurai violence, a pattern of rather permissive child rearing, the absence of deep religious convictions, and the remarkably low ratio of police officers to citizens.

In a 1983 essay I attempted to explain the counterintuitive decline in crime during the period after the Civil War in much the same terms that David H. Bayley had used in a 1976 article dealing with crime in Japan. In both cases, distinctive cultural forces helped restrain individual self-expression. In Japan, these forces subject an individual to the informal social controls of family and neighbors by making him extremely sensitive to the good opinion of others. The controls are of long standing and have so far remained largely intact despite the individualizing tendencies of modernization. In the United States, by contrast, these cultural forces have operated only in certain periods, and when they were effective it was as a result of a herculean effort by scores of voluntary associations specially created for the purpose.

In this country as well as in England, a variety of enterprises—Sunday schools, public schools, temperance movements, religious revivals, YMCAs, the Children's Aid Society—were launched in the first half of the nineteenth century with the common goal of instilling a self-activating, self-regulating, all-purpose inner control. The objects of these efforts were those young men who, freed from the restraints of family life on the farms, had moved to the boardinghouses of the cities in search of economic opportunities. We lack any reliable measure of the effect of these efforts, save one—the extraordinary reduction in the per capita consumption of alcoholic beverages that occurred in America between 1830 (when the temperance efforts began in earnest) and

1850, and that persisted (despite an upturn during and just after the Civil War) for the rest of the century.

We now refer to this period as one in which "Victorian morality" took hold; the term itself, at least as now employed, reflects the condescension with which that ethos has come to be regarded. Modernity, as I have argued elsewhere, involves, at least in elite opinion, replacing the ethic of self-control with that of self-expression. Some great benefits have flowed from this change, including the liberation of youthful energies to pursue new ideas in art, music, literature, politics, and economic enterprise. But the costs are just as real, at least for those young persons who have not already acquired a decent degree of self-restraint and regard for others.

The view that crime has social and cultural as well as economic causes is scarcely new. Hardly any lay person, and only a few scholars, would deny that family and neighborhood affect individual differences in criminality. But what of it? How, as I asked in 1974, might a government remake bad families into good ones, especially on a large scale? How might the government of a free society reshape the core values of its people and still leave them free?

They were good questions then and they remain good ones today. In 1974 there was virtually no reliable evidence that any program seeking to prevent crime by changing attitudes and values had succeeded for any large number of persons. In 1974 I could only urge policymakers to postpone the effort to eliminate the root causes of crime in favor of using those available policy instruments—target hardening, job training, police deployment, court sentences—that might have a marginal effect at a reasonable cost on the commission of crime. Given what we knew then and know now, acting as if crime is the result of individuals freely choosing among competing alternatives may be the best we can do.

Nothing I have written about crime so dismayed some criminologists as this preference for doing what is possible rather than attempting what one wishes were possible. My purpose was to substitute the experimental method for personal ideology; this effort has led some people to suspect I was really trying to substitute my ideology for theirs. Though we all have beliefs that color our views, we ought to try to keep that coloration under control by constant reference to the test of practical effect. What works?

With time and experience we have learned a bit more about what works. There are now some glimmers of hope that certain experimental projects aimed at preparing children for school and equipping parents to cope with unruly offspring may reduce the rate at which these youngsters later commit delinquent acts. Richard J. Herrnstein and I have written about these and related matters in *Crime and Human Nature*. Whether further tests and repeated experiments will confirm that these glimmers emanate from the mother lode of truth and not from fool's gold, no one can yet say. But we know how to find out. If we discover that these ideas can be made to work on a large scale (and not just in the hands of a few gifted practitioners), then we will be able to reduce crime by, in effect, improving character.

Character and Policy

The traditional understanding of politics held that its goal was to improve the character of citizens. The American republic was, as we know, founded on a very different understanding—that of taking human nature pretty much as it was and hoping that personal liberty could survive political action if ambition were made to counteract ambition. The distinctive nature of the American system has led many of its supporters (to say nothing of its critics) to argue that it should be indifferent to character formation. Friend and foe alike are fond of applying to government Samuel Goldwyn's response to the person who asked what message was to be found in his films: if you want to send a message, use Western Union.

Since I yield to no one in my admiration for what the founders created, I do not wish to disagree with their fundamental proposition. But the federal government today is very different from what it was in 1787, 1887, or even 1957. If we wish it to address the problems of family disruption, welfare dependency, crime in the streets, educational inadequacy, or even public finance properly understood, then government, by the mere fact that it defines these states of affairs as problems, acknowledges that human character is in some degree defective and that it intends to alter it. The local governments of village and township always understood this, of course, because they always had responsibility for shaping character. The public school movement, for example, was from the beginning chiefly aimed at moral instruction. The national government could afford to manage its affairs by letting ambition counteract ambition because what was originally at stake in national affairs—creating and maintaining a reasonably secure commercial regime—lent itself naturally to the minimal attentions of a limited government operated and restrained by the reciprocal force of mutual self-interest.

It is easier to acknowledge the necessary involvement of government in character formation than it is to prescribe how this responsibility should be carried out. The essential first step is to acknowledge that at root, in almost every area of important public concern, we are seeking to induce persons to act virtuously, whether schoolchildren, applicants for public assistance, would-be lawbreakers, or voters and public officials. Not only is such conduct desirable in its own right, it appears now to be necessary if large improvements are to be made in those matters we consider problems: schooling, welfare, crime, and public finance.

By virtue, I mean habits of moderate action; more specifically, acting with due restraint on one's impulses, due regard for the rights of others, and reasonable concern for distant consequences. Scarcely anyone favors bad character or a lack of virtue, but it is all too easy to deride a policy of improving character by assuming that this implies a nation of moralizers delivering banal homilies to one another.

Virtue is not learned by precept, however; it is learned by the regular repetition of right actions. We are induced to do the right thing with respect to small matters, and in time we persist in doing the right thing because now we have come to take pleasure in it. By acting rightly with respect to small things, we are more likely to act rightly with respect to large ones. If this view sounds familiar, it should; it is Aristotle's. Let me now quote him directly: "We become just by the practice of just actions, self-controlled by exercising self control."

Seen in this way, the apparent conflict between economic thought and moral philosophy disappears: the latter simply supplies a fuller statement of the uses to which the former can and should be put. We want our families and schools to induce habits of right conduct; most parents and teachers do this by arranging the incentives confronting youngsters in the ordinary aspects of their daily lives so that right action routinely occurs.

What economics neglects is the important subjective consequence of acting in accord with a proper array of incentives: people come to feel pleasure in right action and guilt in wrong action. These feelings of pleasure and pain are not mere "tastes" that policy analysts should take as given; they are the central constraints on human avarice and sloth, the very core of a decent character. A course of action cannot be evaluated simply in terms of its cost-effectiveness, because the consequence of following a given course— if it is followed often enough and regularly enough—is to teach those who follow it what society thinks is right and wrong.

Conscience and character, naturally, are not enough. Rules and rewards must still be employed; indeed, given the irresistible appeal of certain courses of action—such as impoverishing future generations for the benefit of the present one—only some rather draconian rules may suffice. But for most social problems that deeply trouble us, the need is to explore, carefully and experimentally, ways of strengthening the formation of character among the very young. In the long run, the public interest depends on private virtue.

4

The Press at War

Originally published in City Journal, Fall 2006

This essay was published when much of the country, but not President George W. Bush, was about to give up on the war in Iraq. But then Bush adopted the views of General David Petraeus, who wanted to send more troops to Iraq (the "surge") and implement a modern counterinsurgency program that would direct the army to negotiate and live with local populations. The Petraeus plan was successful: deaths of Americans and Iraqis fell sharply and the Iraqi government assumed greater responsibilities. But success comes at a price: the American press has lost interest in Iraq.

We are told by careful pollsters that half of the American people believe that American troops should be brought home from Iraq immediately. This news discourages supporters of our efforts there. Not me, though: I am relieved. Given press coverage of our efforts in Iraq, I am surprised that 90 percent of the public do not want us out right now.

Between January 1 and September 30, 2005, nearly 1,400 stories appeared on the ABC, CBS, and NBC evening news. More than half focused on the costs and problems of the war, four times as many as those that discussed the successes. About 40 percent of the stories reported terrorist attacks; scarcely any reported the triumphs of American soldiers and marines. The few positive stories about progress in Iraq were just a small fraction of all the broadcasts.

In a nonpartisan evaluation of network news broadcasts, the Center for Media and Public Affairs found that during the active war against Saddam Hussein, 51 percent of the reports about the conflict were negative. Six months after the land battle ended, 77 percent were negative; at around the time of the 2004 general election, 89 percent were negative; by the spring of 2006, 94 percent were negative. This decline in media support for the war was much faster than declines during Korea or Vietnam.

Naturally, some of the hostile commentary reflects the nature of reporting. When every news outlet struggles to grab and hold an audience, no one should be surprised that journalists emphasize bloody events. To some degree, the press covers Iraq in much the same way that it covers America, where it highlights conflict, shootings, bombings, hurricanes, tornadoes, and corruption.

But the war coverage does not reflect merely an interest in conflict. People who oppose the entire War on Terror run much of the national press, and they go to great lengths to make waging it difficult. Thus the *New York Times* ran a front-page story about President Bush's allowing, without court warrants, electronic monitoring of phone calls between overseas terrorists and people inside the United States. On the heels of this, the *Times* reported that the FBI had been conducting a top-secret program to monitor radiation levels around U.S. Muslim sites, including mosques. And then both the *New York Times* and the *Los Angeles Times* ran stories about America's effort to monitor foreign banking transactions in order to frustrate terrorist plans. The revelation of this secret effort came five years after a *New York Times* editorial had recommended that precisely such a program be started.

Virtually every government official consulted on these matters urged the press not to run the stories because they endangered secret and important tasks. The press ran them anyway. The media suggested that the National Security Agency surveillance might be illegal, but since we do not know exactly what kind of surveillance has been undertaken, we cannot be clear about its legal basis. No one should assume that the 1978 Foreign Intelligence Surveillance Act requires the president to obtain warrants from the special FISA court before he can monitor foreign intelligence contacts. Though the Supreme Court has never decided this issue, the lower federal courts, almost without exception, have held that "the Executive Branch need not always obtain a warrant for foreign intelligence surveillance."

Nor is it obvious that FISA defines all of the president's authority. Two assistant attorneys general have argued that when the president believes a statute unconstitutionally limits his powers, he has the right not to obey it unless the Supreme Court directs him otherwise. This action would be proper even if the president had signed into law the bill limiting his authority. I know: you are thinking, "That is just what the current Justice Department would say." In fact, these opinions were written in the Clinton administration by assistant attorneys general Walter Dellinger and Randolph Moss.

The president may have such power either because it inheres in his position as commander in chief or because Congress passed a law authorizing him to use "all necessary and appropriate force" against nations or people that directed or aided the attacks of 9/11. Surveillance without warrants may be just such "appropriate force." In any event, presidents before Bush have issued executive orders authorizing searches without warrants, and Jamie Gorelick, once Clinton's deputy attorney general and later a member of the 9/11 Commission, said that physical searches may be done without a court order in foreign intelligence cases. Such searches may well have prevented new terrorist attacks; if they are blocked in the future, no doubt we will see a demand for a new commission charged with criticizing the president for failing to prevent an attack.

The conspirators in the plot to blow up commercial aircraft in flight, arrested in London in 2006, were traced through money transactions that began in Pakistan and through American intercepts of their electronic chatter. Neither the *New York Times* nor the ACLU was able to prevent the British from gaining access to these things. But they would have tried to prevent them if they had been based in London.

Suppose the current media posture about American military and security activities had been in effect during World War II. It is easy to imagine that happening. By the 1930s, after all, the well-connected America First Committee had been arguing for years about the need for America to stay out of "Europe's wars." Aware of these popular views, the House of Representatives extended the draft by only a one-vote margin in 1941. Women in black crowded the entrance to the Senate, arguing against extending the draft. Several hundred students at Harvard and Yale, including future Yale leader Kingman Brewster and future American president Gerald Ford, signed statements saying that they would never go to war. Everything was in place for a media attack on the Second World War. Here is how it might have sounded if today's customs were in effect:

December 1941: Though the press supports America's going to war against Japan after Pearl Harbor, several editorials want to know why we didn't prevent the attack by selling Japan more oil. Others criticize us for going to war with two nations that had never attacked us, Germany and Italy.

October 1942: The *New York Times* runs an exclusive story about the British effort to decipher German messages at a hidden site at Bletchley Park in England. One op-ed writer criticizes this effort, quoting Henry Stimson's statement that gentlemen do not read one another's mail. Because the Bletchley Park code cracking helped us find German submarines before they attacked, successful U-boat attacks increase once the Germans, knowing of the program, change their code.

January 1943: After President Roosevelt and Prime Minister Churchill call for the unconditional surrender of the Axis powers, several newspapers criticize them for having closed the door to a negotiated settlement. The press quotes several senators complaining that the unconditional surrender policy will harm the peace process.

May 1943: A big-city newspaper reveals the existence of the Manhattan Project and describes its effort to build atomic weapons. The article quotes several distinguished scientists lamenting the creation of such a terrible weapon. After General Leslie Groves testifies before a congressional committee, the press lambastes him for wasting money, ignoring scientific opinion, and imperiling the environment by building plants at Hanford and Oak Ridge.

December 1944: The German counterattack against the Allies in the Ardennes yields heavy American losses in the Battle of the Bulge. The press gives splashy coverage to the Democratic National Committee chairman's assertion that the war cannot be won. A member of the House, a former marine, urges that our troops be sent to Okinawa.

August 1945: After President Truman authorizes dropping the atomic bomb on Japan, many newspapers urge his impeachment.

Thankfully, though, the press did not cover World War II the way it has covered Iraq. What caused this profound change? Like many liberals and conservatives, I believe that our Vietnam experience created new media attitudes that have continued down to the present. Some reporters began their coverage supportive of America's role in Vietnam, but that view did not last long. Many people will recall the CBS television program, narrated by Morley Safer, about U.S. Marines using cigarette lighters to torch huts in Cam Ne in 1965. Many will remember the picture of a South Vietnamese officer shooting a captured Vietcong through the head. Hardly anyone can forget the story that ran after a journalist reported that American troops had killed many residents of My Lai.

Undoubtedly, similar events occurred in World War II, but the press didn't cover them. In Vietnam, however, key reporters thought that the Cam Ne story was splendid. David Halberstam said that it "legitimized pessimistic reporting" and would show that "there was something terribly wrong going on out there." Film of the event, he wrote, shattered American "innocence" and raised questions about "who we were."

The changes in media attitudes came to a head in January 1968, during the Tet holiday, when Communist forces launched a major attack on South Vietnamese cities. According to virtually every competent observer, these forces met a sharp defeat, but American press accounts described Tet instead as a major Communist victory. *Washington Post* reporter Peter Braestrup later published a book on the failure of the press to report the Tet Offensive accurately. His summary: "Rarely has contemporary crisis-journalism turned out, in retrospect, to have veered so widely from reality."

Even as the facts became clearer, the press did not correct its false report that the North Vietnamese had won the campaign. When NBC News producer Robert Northshield was asked at the end of 1968 whether the network should air a news show indicating that American and South Vietnamese troops had won, he rejected the idea, because Tet was already "established in the public's mind as a defeat, and therefore it was an American defeat."

In the opinion of Braestrup, the news failure resulted not from ideology but from economic and managerial constraints on the press—and in his view it had no material effect on American public opinion. But others do not share his view. When Douglas Kinnard questioned more than one hundred American generals who served in Vietnam, 92 percent said that newspaper coverage was often irresponsible or disruptive, and 96 percent said that television coverage on balance lacked context and was sensational or counterproductive.

An analysis of CBS's Vietnam coverage in 1972 and 1973 supports their views. The Institute for American Strategy found that, of about eight hundred references to American policy and behavior, 81 percent were critical. Of 164 references to North Vietnamese policy and behavior, 57 percent were supportive. Another study, by a scholar skeptical about the extent of media influence, showed that televised editorial comments before Tet were favorable to our presence by a ratio of four to one; after Tet, they were two to one against the American government's policy. Opinion polls taken in 1968 suggest that before the press reports on the Tet Offensive, 28 percent of the public identified themselves as doves; by March, after the offensive was over, 42 percent said they were doves.

Sociologist James D. Wright directly measured the impact of press coverage by comparing the support for the war among white people of various social classes who read newspapers and news magazines with the support found among those who did not look at these periodicals very much. By 1968, when most news magazines and newspapers had changed from supporting the war to opposing it, backing for the war collapsed among upper-middle-class readers of news stories, from about two-thirds who supported it in 1964 to about one-third who supported it in 1968. Strikingly, opinion did not shift much among working-class voters, no matter whether they read these press accounts or not. Affluent people who read the press apparently have more changeable opinions than ordinary folks. Public opinion may not have changed much, but elite opinion changed greatly.

There are countless explanations for why the media produced so many stories skeptical of or hostile to American military involvement in Vietnam. But many of these explanations are largely myths.

First myth: press hostility was a function of changes in media technology. Vietnam was the first war in which television was available to a mass audience, and, as both critics and admirers of TV unite in saying, television brings the war home in often unsettling images. But the Second World War also brought the struggle home through Pathé and Movietone newsreels, shown in thousands of theaters nationwide at a time when Americans went to the movies remarkably often. Moreover, television accounts between 1962 and 1968 were not critical of the American effort in Vietnam, and public support for the war then actually increased. Hence television cannot account for the change in media attitudes.

Second myth: the media's skepticism about the war in Vietnam emerged because the war was conducted without censorship. The press, with trivial exceptions, could report anything it wanted. Moreover, the absence of a formal declaration of war made it possible for several Americans, including important journalists, to travel to Hanoi, where they made statements about conditions there that often parroted the North Vietnamese party line. But the censorship rules in the Second World War and in Korea, jointly devised by the press and the government, aimed at precluding premature disclosure of military secrets, such as the location of specific combat units and plans for military attacks; they did not constrain journalists' stance on what they reported. The media problem in Vietnam was not the disclosure of secrets but the conveying of an attitude.

Third myth: the press did not report military matters with adequate intelligence and context—did not report sympathetically—because few, if any, journalists had any military training. But that has always been the case. One veteran reporter, S. L. A. Marshall, put the real difference this way: once upon a time, "the American correspondent . . . was an American first, a correspondent second." But in Vietnam, that attitude shifted. An older journalist in Vietnam, who had covered the Second World War, lamented the bitter divisions among the reporters in Saigon, where there were "two camps": "those who wanted to win the war and those who wanted to lose it." The new reporters filed exciting, irreverent copy, which made it to the front pages; the veteran reporters' copy ended up buried way in back.

In place of these three myths, we should consider three much more plausible explanations for the media's attitude toward the war: the first is the weak and ambivalent political leadership that American presidents brought to Vietnam; the second is the existence in the country of a vocal radical movement; and the third is the change that has occurred in the control of media organizations.

First, Presidents Kennedy and Johnson both wanted to avoid losing Vietnam without waging a major war in Asia. Kennedy tried to deny that Americans were fighting. A cable that his administration sent in 1962 instructed diplomats and soldiers never to imply to reporters any "all-out U.S. involvement." Other messages stressed that "this is not a U.S. war." When David Halberstam of the *New York Times* wrote stories criticizing the South Vietnamese government, Kennedy tried to have him fired because he was calling attention to a war that we did not want to admit we were fighting.

Johnson was willing to say that we were fighting, but without any cost and with rosy prospects for an early victory. He sought to avoid losing by a variety of contradictory efforts: he appeased doves (by bombing halts and peace feelers), satisfied hawks (with more troops and more bombing), and controlled the tactical details of the war from the Oval Office. After the Cam Ne report from Morley Safer, Johnson called the head of CBS and berated him in language I will not repeat here.

When Richard Nixon became president, he wanted to end the war by pulling out American troops, and he did so. None of the three presidents wanted to win, but all wanted to report "progress." All three administrations instructed military commanders always to report gains and rely on suspect body counts as a way of measuring progress. The press quickly understood that they could not trust politicians or high-level military officers.

Second, unlike either World War II or the Korean conflict, the Vietnam War saw the rise of a radical peace movement in America, much of it growing out of the New Left. There has been domestic opposition to most of our wars (Karlyn Bowman and I have estimated the size of the "peace party" to be about one-fifth of the electorate), but to this latent public resistance was added a broad critique of American society that opposed the war not only as a wrong policy but as immoral and genocidal—and as a threat to college students' exemption from the draft. Famous opponents of the war traveled to Hanoi to report on North Vietnam. Attorney General Ramsey Clark said that there was neither crime nor internal conflict there. Father Daniel Berrigan described the North Vietnamese people as having a "naïve faith in human goodness." Author Mary McCarthy said these folks had "grace" because they lacked any sense of "alienation."

I repeated for the Iraq War the analysis that Professor Wright had done of the impact of the media on public opinion during the Vietnam War. Using 2004 poll data, I found a similar effect: Americans who rarely watched television news about the 2004 political campaign were much more supportive of the war in Iraq than were those who watched a great deal of TV news. And the falloff in support was greatest for those with a college education.

The third plausible explanation for the media's attitude toward the Vietnam War is that by the time of the war, control of the press had shifted away from owners and publishers to editors and reporters. During the Spanish-American War, the sensationalist press, led by Joseph Pulitzer's

New York World and *St. Louis Post-Dispatch*, William Randolph Hearst's *New York Journal*, and Joseph Medill's *Chicago Tribune*, actively supported the war. Hearst felt, perhaps accurately, that he had helped cause it. His New York paper printed this headline: How do you like the Journal's war? Even the *New York Times* supported the Spanish-American War, editorializing that the Anti-Imperialist League was treasonable and later that the Filipinos "have chosen a bloody way to demonstrate their incapacity for self-government."

Today, strong owners are almost all gone. When Henry Luce died, *Time* magazine's support for an assertive American foreign policy died with him. William Paley had worked hard to make CBS a supporter of the Vietnam War, but he could not prevent Walter Cronkite from making his famous statement on the evening news show of February 19, 1968: the war had become a "stalemate" that had to be ended, and so we must "negotiate." On hearing these remarks, President Johnson decided that the country would no longer support the war and that he should not run for reelection. Over three decades later, Cronkite made the same mistake: we must, he said, get out of Iraq now.

There are still some family owners, such as the Sulzbergers, who exercise control over their newspapers, but they have moved politically left. Ken Auletta has described Arthur Sulzberger, Jr., as a man who has "leaned to the left"; but "leaned" understates the matter. Sulzberger was a passionate opponent of the war in Vietnam and was arrested more than once at protest rallies. When he became publisher in 1997, he chose the liberal Howell Raines to control the editorial page and make it, Sulzberger said, a "more assertive, populist page."

Other media companies, once run by their founders and principal owners, are now run by professional managers who report to directors interested in profits, not policy. Policy is the province of the editors and reporters, who are governed by their personal views, many of them acquired not from having once covered the police beat but from having been to college. By 1978, 93 percent of the top reporters and editors had college degrees.

These three factors worked in concert and have carried down to the present. The ambivalent political leadership of three presidents during Vietnam made the press distrust American leaders, even when, as during the Iraq War, political leadership has been strong. The New Left movement in the 1960s and 1970s slowly abandoned many of its slogans but left its legacy in much of the press and Democratic Party elites. The emergence of journalism as a craft independent of corporate owners reinforced these trends. As one journalist wrote, reporters "had come to reject the idea that they were in any sense part of the American 'team.'" This development happened slowly in Vietnam. Journalists reported most events favorably for the American side from August 1965 to January 1968, but that attitude began shifting with press coverage of Senator J. William Fulbright's hostile Senate hearings and climaxed with the Tet Offensive in January 1968. Thereafter, reporters and editors increasingly shared a distrust of government officials, an inclination to look for cover-ups, and a willingness to believe that the government acted out of bad motives.

A watershed of the new attitude is the coverage of the Pentagon Papers by the *New York Times* in 1971. These documents, prepared by high officials under the direction of Defense Secretary Robert McNamara, were leaked to the *Times* by a former State Department staffer, Daniel Ellsberg. The *Times* wrote major stories, supposedly based on the leaked documents, summarizing the history of our Vietnam involvement.

Edward Jay Epstein, a keen-eyed student of journalism, has shown that in crucial respects the *Times*' coverage was at odds with what the documents actually said. The lead of the *Times* story was that in 1964 the Johnson administration decided to bomb North Vietnam. even as the president was publicly saying that he would not do so. In fact, the Pentagon Papers actually said that, in 1964, the White House had rejected the idea of bombing the north. The *Times* went on to assert that American forces had deliberately provoked the alleged attacks on its ships in the Gulf of Tonkin to justify a congressional resolution supporting our war efforts. In fact, the Pentagon Papers said the opposite: there was no evidence that we had provoked whatever attacks may have occurred.

In short, a key newspaper said that politicians had manipulated us into a war by means of deception. This claim, wrong as it was, was part of a chain of reporting and editorializing that helped convince upper-middle-class Americans that the government could not be trusted.

Reporters and editors today are overwhelmingly liberal politically, as studies of press attitudes have repeatedly shown. Should you doubt these findings, recall the statement of Daniel Okrent, public editor at the *New York Times* from 2003 until 2005. Under the headline, Is the

New York Times a liberal newspaper? Okrent's first sentence was, "Of course it is."

What has been at issue is whether media politics affects media writing. Certainly, writing began to show the influence of politics in the Vietnam years. And thereafter, the press could still support an American war waged by a Democratic president. In 1992, for example, newspapers denounced President George H. W. Bush for having ignored the creation of concentration camps in Bosnia, and they supported President Clinton when he ordered bombing raids there and in Kosovo. When one strike killed some innocent refugees, the *New York Times* said that it would be a "tragedy" to "slacken the bombardment." These air attacks violated what passes for international law (under the UN Charter, people can go to war only for immediate self-defense or under UN authorization). But these supposedly "illegal" air raids did not prevent *Times* support. Today, by contrast, the *Times* criticizes our Guantánamo Bay prison camp for being in violation of "international law."

In the Vietnam era, an important restraint on sectarian partisanship still operated: the mass media catered to a mass audience and hence had an economic interest in appealing to as broad a public as possible. Today, however, we are in the midst of a fierce competition among media outlets, with newspapers trying, not very successfully, to survive against twenty-four/seven TV and radio news coverage and the Internet. As a consequence of this struggle, radio, magazines, and newspapers are engaged in niche marketing, seeking to mobilize not a broad market but a specialized one, either liberal or conservative.

Economics reinforces this partisan orientation. Professor James Hamilton has shown that television networks take older viewers for granted but struggle hard to attract high-spending younger ones. Regular viewers tend to be older, male, and conservative, while marginal ones are likely to be younger, female, and liberal. Thus the financial interest that radio and television stations have in attracting these marginal younger listeners and viewers reinforces their ideological interest in catering to a more liberal audience.

Focusing ever more sharply on the mostly bicoastal, liberal elites, and with their more conservative audience lost to Fox News or Rush Limbaugh, mainstream outlets like the *New York Times* have become more nakedly partisan. And during the Iraq War, they have kept up a drumbeat of negativity that has had a big effect on elite and public opinion alike. Thanks to the power of these media organs, reduced but still enormous, many Americans are coming to see the Iraq War as Vietnam redux.

Most of what I have said here is common knowledge. But it is common knowledge about a new period in American journalistic history. Once, powerful press owners dictated what their papers would print, sometimes irresponsibly. But that era of partisan and circulation-building distortions was not replaced by a commitment to objective journalism; it was replaced by a deep suspicion of the American government. That suspicion, fueled in part by the Vietnam and Watergate controversies, means that the government, especially if it is a conservative one, is surrounded by journalists who doubt almost all it says. One obvious result is that since World War II there have been few reports of military heroes; indeed, there have been scarcely any reports of military victories.

This change in the media is not a transitory one; it is unlikely that the media will return to supporting our military when it fights. Journalism, like so much scholarship, now dwells in a postmodern age in which truth is hard to find and statements merely serve someone's interests.

The mainstream media's adversarial stance, both here and abroad, means that whenever a foreign enemy challenges us, he will know that his objective will be to win the battle not on some faraway bit of land but among the people who determine what we read and watch. We won the Second World War in Europe and Japan, but we lost in Vietnam, and are in danger of losing in Iraq and Lebanon in the newspapers, magazines, and television programs we enjoy.

5

Defining the "Peace Party"

(written with Karlyn Bowman)[1]

Originally published in The Public Interest, *Fall 2003*

The peace party in America has existed for at least half a century, but during the war in Iraq it became a major national force. Though Democrats and Republicans disagreed about our involvement in Korea and Vietnam, the partisan differences were not huge. During the Iraq War, they became decisive. The great majority of Democrats opposed our efforts there and a majority of Republicans supported them. So strong did the peace party become that it was a major factor in the election of Barack Obama and worked hard, though not always successfully, to shape his diplomacy. At the very least it succeeded in helping the president apologize for America's "mistakes."

———— ✇ ————

When the war in Iraq was at its media peak, about one-fifth of Americans strongly opposed our being there. Surveys taken in December 2002 showed that 15 to 20 percent of the public resolutely opposed the war three months before it began, and the numbers remained about as high in April 2003, after the war had been underway for a couple of weeks. While the level of support increased after the war began, the onset of fighting did not budge the war's strongest opponents. This "peace party" became known to the American public through antiwar protests and demonstrations, but media coverage of these events did not tell us much about the composition of this group. Who makes up the peace party? How many Americans have joined its ranks? And how do their numbers compare with the numbers opposing past military conflicts?

Answering these questions is quite difficult both because the Iraq War was unlike conflicts of the past and because there are limits to how much we can learn from polling data. Most polls about the war do not provide those surveyed with information about the events under review. Respondents are left to make their own conjectures regarding such questions as the number of troops involved, likely casualties, financial costs, and the aftereffects of the war. Press coverage during wartime offers conflicting accounts of events, and both pro-war and antiwar sentiments may reflect these uncertainties. In what follows, we shall try to discover the defining characteristics of America's peace party by limiting our analysis to those who were strongly antiwar.

An Exceptional Case?

Opposition to involvement in the Korean and Vietnam wars began at roughly the same level as opposition to our fighting in Iraq: around one-fifth of the American public opposed joining the war in Korea in July 1950, and about one-quarter opposed sending troops to help South Vietnam in the second half of 1965. But neither of these wars progressed as rapidly or as successfully as the invasion of Iraq, and opposition to them grew. In mid-1951, after China had entered the war, public opposition to the Korean War rose to over 40 percent. By late 1967, opposition to our military efforts in Vietnam increased to around 45 percent.

Despite the rapid defeat of Saddam Hussein's army (the ground war took three weeks compared to three years in Korea and twelve in Vietnam), the number of Americans voicing strong opposition never diminished. The war to defeat the Taliban regime in Afghanistan was more popular. Opponents of that effort never exceeded one-tenth of the public, and were often a much smaller proportion than this. There are probably two reasons: our attack in Afghanistan came not long after the terrorist assaults of September 11, and for a long time large numbers of ground forces were never committed there. In the public's eye, our response to the terrorist attacks was both morally justified and relatively costless. But when pollsters asked people about the prospect of sending "significant numbers of U.S. ground troops" to Afghanistan, opposition more than doubled.

Those who were strongly opposed to our invasion of Iraq were indifferent to the role of the United Nations. About one-fifth opposed our military activity regardless of whether the United States had UN support or Iraq had weapons of mass destruction. A Gallup poll taken in early April 2003 showed that 15 percent of the respondents opposed the war "even if the U.S. finds conclusive evidence that Iraq has weapons of mass destruction." One tenth of all voters said that we should "never" have attacked Iraq. In another poll, about one-tenth of all Americans said that they are "antiwar in general." And in yet another public opinion survey conducted in March 2003, almost one-fifth said that war is "never morally justified."

The peace party's composition may depend in part on which political party is in power. When we fought in Korea and Vietnam, two wars begun under Democratic presidents, political scientist John Mueller found that Democrats supported the war more than Republicans did. Democratic opponents of the war in Vietnam began to equal or outnumber Republican critics only after Richard Nixon became president in 1969. We have no way of knowing whether Nixon's presence caused this shift (after all, the war had made critics among both Republicans and Democrats by that time), but it is striking that Democratic opposition shot up around the middle of 1969, while Republican opposition remained relatively constant.

Party Politics

The peace party today cannot be explained by age, income, or education. In a Gallup analysis of polls conducted in January and March of 2003, majorities regardless of age, income, or education supported the Iraq war, though the majorities were not equally large. One exception to this picture is that large numbers of people with advanced degrees tended to be implacable opponents of the war. Schooling did not make a difference, unless you had acquired a lot of it. Indeed, postgraduates are one of the most reliably liberal groups in America today. But there are large differences in support for and opposition to the war that center on political party, ideology, and race.

Democrats were twice as likely to oppose the war as Republicans, and blacks were more opposed to it than whites by almost the same margin. Taken as a whole, women were somewhat more opposed than men, though this difference varied depending on whether the women had children, worked, or lived in rural areas. Mothers were less opposed than other women, and stay-at-home mothers were less opposed than working ones.

Party differences have deepened over the years. In a recent paper delivered at Princeton University, political scientist Gary Jacobson noted that, before the terrorist attacks of September 11, the gap between Democratic and Republican support of President Bush was wider than it has been for any prior president, including Bill Clinton. Before September 11, 88 percent of self-identified Republicans supported Bush; only 31 percent of self-identified Democrats did. This fifty-seven-point gap was the largest Jacobson had ever found. After September 11, support for President Bush sharply increased, but the gap in party attitudes toward Iraq remained wide. In March 2003, 57 percent of liberal Democrats opposed military action against Iraq, while 95 percent of conservative Republicans supported it.

Ideology Matters

Partisan opposition to the war probably reflects the higher level of ideological conflict that exists among voters today. That conflict makes it possible for antiwar candidates such as Howard Dean to run effective campaigns for the Democratic presidential nomination. According to Matt Bai, writing in the *New York Times Magazine*, when Dean's campaign began he was getting about fifty e-mail messages of support a day. After making clear his opposition to the war in Iraq, e-mail messages to his Web site shot up to about two thousand a day. In the second quarter of 2003, Dean raised significantly more money than his rivals, with over $4 million coming through his Web site. Clearly, Dean has energized the liberal, antiwar wing of the Democratic Party. Some of its members, such as Harvard law professor Christopher Edley, were delighted by a candidate who is "unashamed and unembarrassed to express what we stand for." Others, such as Bruce Reed, president of the Democratic Leadership Council, worry that if Dean pulls the party too far to the left "it'll be a disaster for the party and the country."

Greater ideological polarization may also reflect lingering resentments over Clinton's impeachment and the view of many Democrats that Bush "stole" the 2000 presidential election. But we suspect that deeper forces are at work. For one, votes in Congress have become markedly more partisan over the years. In 1970, about one-third of all House and Senate votes pitted the majority of one party against the majority of the other, but by 1998 more than half of the votes were of this sort. In 1970, about 70 percent of each party's congressional members voted on partisan lines when a majority of one party was opposed by a majority of the other. In 1998, that number had risen to 90 percent. When President Clinton was impeached, 98 percent of House Republicans voted for at least one of the four impeachment articles, while 98 percent of House Democrats voted against all four. Even in House districts where most voters opposed impeachment, almost all Republican members voted in favor of it.

There are many reasons why Congress is more polarized politically than it once was. Drawing district lines to reward incumbents has protected most Democrats and Republicans from the risk of any serious electoral opposition. Party leaders are more ideological. But beneath all of this is the possibility that the voters themselves are more polarized. Both Gary Jacobson and fellow political scientist Larry Bartels have produced data suggesting that, in comparison to twenty or thirty years ago, voters today are more comfortable with ideological labels and more ready to identify with a particular party on the basis of its ideology. This is especially true of more educated voters. Anyone who doubts these findings need only listen to radio talk shows or compare Fox News with public-broadcasting news to encounter daily evidence of a profound market segmentation in the media, a segmentation that could exist only if there were large numbers of ideological voters to whom different programs could appeal.

One of the results of this polarization is the existence of a large group of hawkish voters who favor a muscular American military policy and a smaller but intense group of dovish ones who oppose military action under almost any circumstances. These groups—the "war party" and "peace party"—correspond closely to party identification.

There are parallels between the peace party here and the ones we find abroad. When the Pew Research Center in 2003 polled voters in twenty nations, it found that people having a "somewhat" or "very" unfavorable attitude toward the United States made up about one-fifth of the public in friendly countries such as Australia, Canada, Great Britain, Israel, Italy, Kuwait, and South Korea. The Pew researchers then asked about these unfavorable views: was it some general problem with America or mostly because of George W. Bush? In sixteen of the twenty cases, the respondents said it was Bush. Now, it is hard to know what this means, but it does suggest that the leader of the country makes a difference. And it reminds us that in those countries most friendly to us, the anti-American party is about the same size as the peace party here.

Black Opinion

A Gallup analysis that combined the results of two polls taken in late March 2003 found that only 28 percent of blacks supported the war, while 68 percent were opposed to it. This is quite different from African-American attitudes in earlier conflicts. John Mueller noticed that from 1950 to 1953, the number of black men who opposed the Korean War was not significantly different from the number of white men or women who opposed it (black women, by contrast, were the most opposed). In the late 1960s, black men displayed roughly the same level of opposition to the war in Vietnam as did white men. Once again, black women were the most opposed.

By 2003, a big change in blacks' attitudes toward war had occurred. Nearly two-thirds of all blacks opposed the war. Opposition was much greater than it had been to Operation Desert Storm twelve years earlier. A Gallup analysis of polls from late March and early April 2003 showed a sharp decline in black support of American military efforts since Kuwait in 1991. Fifty-nine percent of all blacks supported American military involvement in Kuwait; when we invaded Iraq a dozen years later, only 28 percent supported the effort.

The changing influence of race is difficult to explain. Defense Department officials responsible for recruitment regularly survey prospective recruits and conduct focus group interviews in order to measure the "propensity to serve." Among black high school seniors, the willingness to serve decreased significantly after the release of two motion pictures, Boyz n the Hood (1991) and Get on the Bus (1996). In the first of these, a well-known black actor says that the U.S. government is funneling drugs into black communities and argues that the army is no place for a black man. In the second film a character who says positive things about Colin Powell is called an Uncle Tom.

The effect of these films—and of remarks by black antiwar leaders such as Jesse Jackson—was undeniable: in their focus group discussions, black students pointed to these influences as reasons for their negative views of the military. But these effects were temporary. Over the long haul, recruitment of blacks into the military has remained more or less constant. In 2000, about 20 percent of all enlisted recruits were black, with higher numbers in the army than in the other armed services.

Because so few black respondents are found in typical public opinion polls, measuring attitudes among particular groups of blacks is difficult. For the most part, we must rely on the published statements of black leaders. They have made essentially these arguments: that a war in Iraq diverts resources and efforts away from domestic programs that would benefit blacks, and that because blacks are overrepresented in the armed forces, they will in all likelihood be overrepresented among American casualties. More generally, many blacks still believe that President Bush "stole" the election and find his policies on race anathema.

The trouble is that neither of the first two criticisms explains the sharp increase in black opposition to the war in Iraq in comparison with past wars. The wars in Korea, Vietnam, and Kuwait consumed resources that might have been used for domestic programs, but blacks supported these military efforts in spite of it.

Clearly, something has changed. It is possible that blacks have begun to move left on issues of war and peace. They may have decided that support for the wars in Korea and Vietnam gained them few advances in key areas of concern. But though that argument might explain sentiments in the 1950s—a decade during which next to nothing was done to improve race relations—it cannot as easily explain them in 1972 after major civil-rights laws had been passed, school desegregation was underway, and a war on poverty had been launched.

As for the second argument, black Americans have not been greatly over-represented among troops who have died in war. In the Korean conflict, 8.4 percent of deaths were of blacks. In Vietnam, black soldiers made up 11.3 percent of the troops and 12.4 percent of the deaths, hardly a significant difference. In the 1991 Persian Gulf War, blacks were underrepresented among the dead: black soldiers made up 22.8 percent of the troops there but only 17.2 percent of the deaths. The same pattern emerged in Operation Iraqi Freedom: blacks were 22.8 percent of the troops in the area but only 16.5 percent of the military deaths through May 1, 2003.

Nor does the state of the U.S. military itself seem to help us understand why blacks tend not to support the war in Iraq. Political scientists David King and Zachary Karabell point out in their recent book, *The Generation of Trust*, that blacks have made significant progress in achieving racial integration in the military. The military, and especially the army, launched programs that sharply increased the percentage of blacks among senior noncommissioned and commissioned officers. As sociologists Charles Moskos and John Sibley Butler have shown, black soldiers are more satisfied with their jobs than white civilians are with theirs.

One new factor that may well help us understand the shift in black opinion is the widespread dislike of George W. Bush within the black community. The president is indisputably less popular among blacks than President Clinton. "Bush puts forth an agenda seen by black people as antagonistic," according to Elijah Anderson, a black sociologist at the University of Pennsylvania. This perspective explains "a huge amount of the alienation in the black community." Not only did Bush supposedly steal the election, but he did so in a contest in which many black votes in Florida are believed to have gone uncounted, and after having served as the governor of Texas, a state that led the nation in executing prisoners, many of whom were black. But it is also likely that black opinion on some issues, such as foreign and military policy, has simply moved left, just as has happened among Democratic voters generally.

The Peace Candidate

Today's peace party amounts to only about one-fifth of all Americans, but it may enjoy a special position in selecting presidential candidates for the Democratic Party. Primary elections and local caucuses give a special advantage to committed activists. In the Republican Party, this means that antiabortion and progun groups are likely to have more influence in picking candidates than they will in determining the outcome of general elections. In the Democratic Party, proabortion, antigun, and peace activists will also have more influence in selecting candidates than they will in deciding who wins in November's election. Since most contests for a seat in the House of Representatives are essentially uncontested, with one party or the other holding an insurmountable advantage, the identity of the candidate is more important than the outcome of the election. For many Senate seats and for the presidential race, there is much more electoral competition.

Political analyst Charlie Cook cited clear evidence that very liberal Democrats are overrepresented among those likely to vote in primaries. A February 2003 survey showed that 63 percent of likely primary voters favored military action against Saddam Hussein, but about half of Democrats opposed it. "Core Democrats"—that is, liberal Democrats likely to vote in the primaries—were opposed by nearly two-thirds. As Cook observed, while these core Democrats make up only about one-third of the party's members, they are its most active and visible members.

Democratic and Republican candidates with varying views on abortion and guns have won the presidency because the public is divided on these matters. That is not the case as regards war. Democratic senatorial and presidential candidates will have to tread carefully. They will need to be sufficiently critical of war initiatives to win the nomination yet sufficiently supportive of the armed forces to win the general election. The strategy by which this is now being carried out seems clear: criticize the steps leading up to a war (by demanding that the United Nations or our allies support it), but back the troops once war begins.

Whether this stratagem will remain effective is unclear. Peace demonstrators took pains to shun overt displays of anti-American sentiment and made a point of displaying American flags, but most Americans were still put off by their message. Politicians who declare themselves antiwar but say they support our troops will have to explain why they voted against a war that quickly and with remarkably few deaths displaced a monstrous dictator, ended the terror of the Iraqi people, and diminished the support available to terrorist organizations.

Note

1. The authors would like to thank Todd Weiner for his research assistance.

6

Bowling with Others
Originally published in Commentary, *October 2007*

America is a nation of joiners but perhaps, as Robert Putnam argues, Americans'
affinity for joining is on the wane owing to the lure of television, the Internet, and
computer games. Putnam found that states with more "social capital," which
includes a high level of public involvement in voluntary associations, also tend to be
highly tolerant of diversity. But in a new essay he shows that Americans living in
ethnically diverse areas are less likely to join groups than others, and that we are
perhaps less enamored of ethnic diversity than we had thought.

Some people believe that we are losing the attachment to family, friends,
neighbors, and associates that Alexis de Tocqueville once called a defining
characteristic of American life. In his celebrated book, *Bowling Alone* (2000),
the political scientist Robert D. Putnam argued that America, and perhaps the
Western world as a whole, has become increasingly disconnected. We once
bowled in leagues; now we bowl alone. We once flocked to local chapters of
the PTA, the NAACP, or the Veterans of Foreign Wars; now we stay home and
watch television. As a result, we have lost our "social capital"—by which
Putnam means both the associations themselves and the trustworthiness and
reciprocity they encourage. For if tools (physical capital) and training (human
capital) make the modern world possible, social capital is what helps people
find jobs and enables neighborhoods and other small groupings of society to
solve problems, control crime, and foster a sense of community.

In *Bowling Alone*, Putnam devised a scale for assessing the condition of
organizational life in different American states. He looked to such measures
as the density of civic groups, the frequency with which people participate in

them, and the degree to which (according to opinion surveys) people trust one another. Controlling for race, income, education, and the like, he demonstrated that the higher a state's level of social capital, the more educated and affluent are its children, the lower the murder rate, the greater the degree of public health, and the smaller the likelihood of tax evasion. Nor is that all. High levels of social capital, Putnam showed, are associated with such civic virtues as greater tolerance toward women and minorities and stronger support for civil liberties. But all of these good things have been seriously jeopardized by the phenomenon he identified as "bowling alone."

After finishing his book, Putnam was approached by various community foundations to measure the levels of social capital within their own cities. To that end he conducted a very large survey: roughly thirty thousand Americans, living in forty-one communities of different sizes, from Los Angeles to Yakima, Washington, and even rural areas of South Dakota. He published the results this year in a long essay in the academic journal *Scandinavian Political Studies* on the occasion of his having won Sweden's prestigious Johan Skytte Prize.

Putnam's new essay takes an in-depth look not at social capital per se but at how "diversity"—meaning, for this purpose, racial and ethnic differences—affects our lives in society. Such diversity is increasing in this country and many others, if for no other reason than immigration, and so Putnam has tried to find out how it changes the way people feel about their neighbors, the degree of their confidence in local government, their willingness to become engaged in community-wide projects, and their general happiness.

The ethnic and racial diversity that Putnam examines is widely assumed to be very good for us. The more time we spend with people different from us, it is said, the more we will like and trust them. Indeed, diversity is supposed to be so good for us that it has become akin to a national mandate in employment and, especially, in admissions to colleges and universities. When the Supreme Court decided the *Bakke* case in 1978, the leading opinion, signed by Justice Lewis Powell, held that although a university was not allowed to use a strict numerical standard to guarantee the admission of a fixed number of minority students, it could certainly "take race into account," on the theory that a racially diverse student body was desirable both for the school and for society at large.

As a result of this and similar court rulings, not only colleges but many other institutions began invoking the term "diversity" as a justification for programs that gave preferences to certain favored minorities (especially blacks and Hispanics). Opponents of these programs (who felt they violated constitutional standards of equal treatment) were put in the difficult position of appearing to oppose a demonstrated social good. Did not everyone know that our differences make us stronger?

But do they? That is where Putnam's new essay comes in. In the long run, Putnam argues, ethnic and racial diversity in neighborhoods is indeed "an important social asset," because it encourages people to form connections that reduce unproductive forms of ethnocentrism and increase economic growth. In his words, "successful immigrant societies create new forms of social solidarity and dampen the negative effects of diversity by constructing new, more encompassing identities."

Whatever his beliefs about the positive effects of diversity in the long run, however—not only is it a potentially "important social asset," it also confers "many advantages that have little or nothing to do with social capital"— Putnam is a scrupulous and serious scholar (as well as a friend and former colleague at Harvard). In the *short* run, he is frank to acknowledge, the effect of diversity is not positive but rather the opposite. "The more ethnically diverse the people we live around," he writes, "the less we trust them."

Diversity, Putnam concludes on the basis of his findings, makes us "hunker down." Not only do we trust our neighbors less, we have less confidence in local government, a lowered sense of our own political efficacy, fewer close friends, and a smaller likelihood of contributing to charities, cooperating with others, working on a community project, registering to vote—or being happy.

Of course many of these traits can reflect just the characteristics of the people Putnam happened to interview, rather than some underlying condition. Aware of the possibility, Putnam spent a great deal of time "kicking the tires" of his study by controlling statistically for age, ethnicity, education, income or lack of same, homeownership, citizenship, and many other possible influences. But the results did not change. No matter how many individual factors were analyzed, every measure of social well-being suffered in ethnically diverse neighborhoods—and improved in ethnically homogeneous ones.

"Shocking" is the word that one political scientist, Scott Page of the University of Michigan, used to describe the extent of the negative social effects revealed by Putnam's data. Whether Putnam was shocked by the results I cannot say. But they should not have been surprising; others have reported the same thing. The scholars Anil Rupasingha, Stephan J. Goetz, and David Freshwater, for example, found that social capital across American counties, as measured by the number of voluntary associations for every ten thousand people, goes up with the degree of ethnic homogeneity. Conversely, as others have discovered, when ethnic groups are mixed there is weaker social trust, less carpooling, and less group cohesion. And this has held true for some time: people in Putnam's survey who were born in the 1920s display the same attitudes as those born in the 1970s.

Still, Putnam believes that in the long run ethnic heterogeneity will indeed "create new forms of social solidarity." He offers three reasons. First, the American military, once highly segregated, is today anything but that—and yet, in the army and the marines, social solidarity has increased right alongside greater ethnic diversity. Second, churches that were once highly segregated, especially large evangelical ones, have likewise become entirely and peaceably integrated. Third, people who once married only their ethnic kin today marry across ethnic and religious (and, to a lesser degree, racial) lines.

I can offer a fourth example of an institution that has gone from homogeneous to heterogeneous: organized sports. Once, baseball and football teams were made up of only white or only black players; today they, too, are fully integrated. When Jackie Robinson joined the Brooklyn Dodgers in 1947, several teammates objected to playing with him, and many fans heckled him whenever he took the field. Within a few years, however, he and the Dodgers had won a raft of baseball titles, and he was one of the most popular figures in the country. Today such racial and ethnic heckling has virtually disappeared.

Unfortunately, however, the pertinence of the military, religious, or athletic model to life in neighborhoods is very slight. In those three institutions, authority and discipline can break down native hostilities or force them underground. Military leaders proclaim that bigotry will not be tolerated, and they mean it; preachers invoke the word of God to drive home the lesson that prejudice is a sin; sports teams (as with the old Brooklyn Dodgers) point out that anyone who does not want to play with a black or a Jew is free to seek employment elsewhere.

But what authority or discipline can anyone bring to neighborhoods? They are places where people choose to live, out of either opportunity or necessity. Walk the heterogeneous streets of Chicago or Los Angeles and you will learn about organized gangs and other social risks. Nor are these confined to poor areas: Venice is a small neighborhood in Los Angeles where several movie stars live and where many homes sell for over $1 million, but the Shoreline Crips and the V-13 gangs operate there.

In many neighborhoods, ethnic differences are often seen as threats. If blacks or Hispanics, for whatever reason, are more likely to join gangs or commit crimes, then whites living in a neighborhood with many blacks or Hispanics will tend to feel uneasy. (There are, of course, exceptions: some, especially among the well-educated, prefer diversity even with its risks.) Even where everyone is equally poor or equally threatened by crime, people exhibit less trust if their neighborhood is ethnically diverse than if it is homogeneous.

Of Putnam's reasons for thinking that ethnic heterogeneity will contribute to social capital in the long run, only one is compelling: people are indeed voluntarily marrying across ethnic lines. But the paradoxical effect of this trend is not to preserve but to blunt ethnic identity, to the point where it may well reduce the perception of how diverse a neighborhood actually is. In any case, the fact remains that diversity and improved solidarity have gone hand in hand only in those institutions characterized by enforced authority and discipline.

The legal scholar Peter H. Schuck has written an important book on this issue. In *Diversity in America* (2003), he examines three major efforts by judges and government officials to require racial and income diversity in neighborhoods. One of them banned income discrimination in the sale and rental of housing in New Jersey towns. Another enabled blacks who were eligible for public housing to move into private rental units in the Chicago suburbs. In the third, a federal judge attempted to diversify residential patterns in the city of Yonkers, New York, by ordering the construction of public housing in middle-class neighborhoods selected by him.

Although the Chicago project may have helped minorities to enter communities where they had never lived, the New Jersey and Yonkers initiatives had little effect. As Schmuck writes, "Neighborhoods are complex, fragile, organic societies whose dynamics outsiders cannot readily understand, much less control." A court can and should strike down racist public policies, but when it goes beyond this and tries to mandate "diversity," it will sooner or later discover that it "cannot conscript the housing market to do its bidding."

Taking a different approach, Thomas Schelling, a Nobel laureate in economics, has shown in a stimulating essay that neighborhood homogeneity and even segregation may result from small, defensible human choices that cannot themselves be called racist. In fact, such choices can lead to segregation even when the people making them expressly intend the opposite. Suppose, Schelling writes, that blacks and whites alike wish to live in a neighborhood that is (for example) half-white and half-black. If one white family should come to think that other white families in the neighborhood prefer a community that is three-fourths white, and may move out for that reason, the first white family is itself likely to move out in search of its own half-white, half-black preference. There is no way to prevent this.

Schelling's analysis casts a shadow of doubt on Putnam's own policy suggestions for reducing the disadvantages and stimulating the benefits of ethnic heterogeneity. Those suggestions are investing more heavily in playgrounds, schools, and athletic fields that different groups can enjoy together; extending national aid to local communities; encouraging churches to reach out to new immigrants; and expanding public support for the teaching of English.

The first recommendation is based on the implicit assumption that Schelling is wrong and on the even more dubious assumption that playgrounds, schools, and athletic fields—things Putnam did not measure in his survey—will increase the benefits of diversity even when age, income, and education do not. The second is empty: Putnam does not say what kind of aid will produce the desired effects. If he is thinking of more housing, Schuck has already shown that housing is not usually a route to increased diversity. If he is thinking of education, recall that in the 1970s federal judges imposed forced busing in an effort to integrate schools. It was an intensely unpopular strategy, both among those whose children were being bused and among those in the neighborhoods receiving the bused children.

The third proposal, encouraging outreach by churches, might well make a difference, but how do we go about it? Require people to attend an evangelical church? Would Robert Putnam attend? I suspect not. And as for the final recommendation, teaching English at public expense to everyone, it is a very good idea—provided one could break the longstanding attachment of the education establishment to bilingual instruction.

Whether we should actually seek to transform the situation described by Putnam's data is another question. I do not doubt that both diversity and social capital are important, or that many aspects of the latter have declined, though perhaps not so much as Putnam suspects. But as his findings indicate, there is no reason to suppose that the route to the latter runs through the former. In fact, strong families living in neighborhoods made up of families with shared characteristics seem much more likely to bring their members into the associational life Putnam favors. Much as we might value both heterogeneity and social capital, assuming that the one will or should encourage the other may be a form of wishful thinking.

That is because morality and rights arise from different sources. As I tried to show in *The Moral Sense* (1993), morality arises from sympathy among like-minded persons: first the family, then friends and colleagues. Rights, on the other hand, grow from convictions about how we ought to manage relations with people not like us, convictions that are nourished by education, religion, and experience.

People who celebrate diversity (and its parallel, multiculturalism) are endorsing only one part of what it means to be a complete human being, neglecting morality (and its parallel, group and national pride). Just as we cannot be whole persons if we deny the fundamental rights of others, so we cannot be whole persons if we live in ways that discourage decency, cooperation, and charity.

In every society, people must arrange for trade-offs between desirable but mutually inconsistent goals. James Madison, in his famous *Federalist No. 10*, pointed to just this sort of trade-off when he made the case for a large national government that would ensure the preservation of those individual rights and liberties that are at risk in small communities. When it comes to the competing values of diversity and social capital, as when it comes to other arrangements in a democracy, balance is all.

7

How Divided Are We?

Originally published in Commentary, *February 2006*

No one doubts that Congress is deeply polarized along party lines, but scholars do disagree about whether the public at large is polarized. I believe that the public is deeply divided. In 2006, 76 percent of Democrats said we should have stayed out of Iraq, while 71 percent of Republicans said we were right to invade. This split was unprecedented in American history. In this essay I try to explain why it has happened.

The 2004 election left our country deeply divided over whether our country is deeply divided. For some, America is indeed a polarized nation, perhaps more so today than at any time in living memory. In this view, yesterday's split between lovers and haters of Bill Clinton has given way to today's even more acrimonious split between Americans who detest George Bush and Americans who detest John Kerry, and similar divisions will persist as long as angry liberals and angry conservatives continue to confront each other across the political abyss. Others, however, believe that most Americans are moderate centrists, who, although disagreeing over partisan issues in 2004, harbor no deep ideological hostility. I take the former view.

By polarization I do not have in mind partisan disagreements alone. These have always been with us. Since popular voting began in the nineteenth century, scarcely any winning candidate has received more than 60 percent of the vote, and very few losers have received less than 40 percent. Inevitably, Americans will differ over who should be in the White House. But this does not necessarily mean they are polarized.

By polarization I mean something else: an intense commitment to a candidate, a culture, or an ideology that sets people in one group definitively apart from people in another, rival group. Such a condition is revealed when a candidate for public office is regarded by a competitor and his supporters not simply as wrong but as corrupt or wicked; when one way of thinking about the world is assumed to be morally superior to any other way; when one set of political beliefs is considered to be entirely correct and a rival set wholly wrong. In extreme form, as defined by Richard Hofstadter in *The Paranoid Style in American Politics* (1965), polarization can entail the belief that the other side is in thrall to a secret conspiracy using devious means to obtain control over society. Today's versions might go like this: "Liberals employ their dominance of the media, the universities, and Hollywood to enforce a radically secular agenda"; or, "conservatives, working through the religious Right and the big corporations, conspired with their hired neo-con advisers to invade Iraq for the sake of oil."

A Closer Look at the Divisions

Polarization is not new to this country. It is hard to imagine a society more divided than ours was in 1800, when pro-British, procommerce New Englanders supported John Adams for the presidency while pro-French, proagriculture southerners backed Thomas Jefferson. One sign of this hostility was the passage of the Alien and Sedition Acts in 1798; another was that in 1800, just as in 2000, an extremely close election was settled by a struggle in one state (New York in 1800, Florida in 2000).

The fierce contest between Abraham Lincoln and George McClellan in 1864 signaled another national division, this one over the conduct of the Civil War. But thereafter, until recently, the nation ceased to be polarized in that sense. Even in the half-century from 1948 to (roughly) 1996, marked as it was by sometimes strong expressions of feeling over whether the presidency should go to Harry Truman or Thomas Dewey, to Dwight Eisenhower or Adlai Stevenson, to John F. Kennedy or Richard Nixon, to Nixon or Hubert Humphrey, and so forth, opinion surveys do not indicate widespread detestation of one candidate or the other, or of the people who supported him.

Now they do. Today, many Americans and much of the press regularly speak of President George W. Bush as a dimwit, a charlatan, or a knave. A former Democratic presidential candidate has asserted that Bush "betrayed" America by launching a war designed to benefit his friends and corporate backers. A senior Democratic senator has characterized administration policy as a series of "lies, lies, and more lies" and has accused Bush of plotting a "mindless, needless, senseless, and reckless" war. From the other direction, similar expressions of popular disdain have been directed at Senator John Kerry (and before him at President Bill Clinton); if you have not heard them, that may be because (unlike many of my relatives) you do not live in Arkansas or Texas or other locales where the *New York Times* is not read. In these places, Kerry is widely spoken of as a scoundrel.

In the 2004 presidential election, over two-thirds of Kerry voters said they were motivated explicitly by the desire to defeat Bush. By early 2005, President Bush's approval rating, which stood at 94 percent among Republicans, was only 18 percent among Democrats — the largest such gap in the history of the Gallup poll. These data, moreover, were said to reflect a mutual revulsion between whole geographical sections of the country, the so-called red (Republican) states versus the so-called blue (Democratic) states. As summed up by the distinguished social scientist who writes humor columns under the name of Dave Barry, residents of red states are "ignorant racist fascist knuckle-dragging NASCAR-obsessed cousin-marrying road-kill-eating tobacco-juice-dribbling gun-fondling religious fanatic rednecks," while blue-state residents are "godless unpatriotic pierced-nose Volvo-driving France-loving leftwing Communist latte-sucking tofu-chomping holistic-wacko neurotic vegan weenie perverts."

To be sure, other scholars differ with Dr. Barry. To them, polarization, although a real enough phenomenon, is almost entirely confined to a small number of political elites and members of Congress. In *Culture War?* (2004), which bears the subtitle *The Myth of a Polarized America*, Morris Fiorina of Stanford argues that policy differences between voters in red and blue states are really quite small, and that most are in general agreement even on issues like abortion and homosexuality.

But the extent of polarization cannot properly be measured by the voting results in red and blue states. Many of these states are in fact deeply divided internally between liberal and conservative areas, and gave the nod to one candidate or the other by only a narrow margin. In California, for example, liberals are concentrated along the coastline and conservatives are found inland. California votes for Democratic presidential candidates by a modest margin, but that does not mean that California voters are just like those in Tennessee who usually vote Republican by a small margin. Coastal liberals in California are well to the left of liberals in Tennessee, just as Tennessee conservatives are well to the right of their counterparts in California. Inferring the views of individual citizens from the gross results of presidential balloting is a questionable procedure.

Nor does Fiorina's analysis capture the very real and very deep division over an issue like abortion. Between 1973, when *Roe v. Wade* was decided, and now, he writes, there has been no change in the degree to which people will or will not accept any one of six reasons to justify an abortion: (1) the woman's health is endangered; (2) she became pregnant because of a rape; (3) there is a strong chance of a fetal defect; (4) the family has a low income; (5) the woman is not married; (6) and the woman simply wants no more children. Fiorina may be right about that. Nevertheless, only about 40 percent of all Americans will support abortion for any of the last three reasons in his series, while over 80 percent will support it for one or another of the first three.

In other words, almost all Americans accept abortion in the case of maternal emergency, but fewer than half where it is simply a matter of the mother's preference. That split—a profoundly important one—has remained in place for over three decades, *and* it affects how people vote. In 2000 and again in 2004, 70 percent of those who thought abortion should always be legal voted for Al Gore or John Kerry, while over 70 percent of those who thought it should always be illegal voted for George Bush.

Division is just as great over other high-profile issues. Polarization over the war in Iraq, for example, is more pronounced than any war-related controversy in at least a half-century. In the fall of 2005, according to Gallup, 81 percent of Democrats but only 20 percent of Republicans thought the war in Iraq was a mistake. During the Vietnam War, by contrast, itself a famously contentious cause, there was more unanimity across party lines, whether for or against: in late 1968 and early 1969, about equal numbers of Democrats and Republicans thought the intervention there was a mistake. Although attitudes toward the war in Korea reflected a partisan split—in early 1951,

44 percent of Democrats and 61 percent of Republicans thought the war was a mistake—the split was nowhere near as large as the one over our present campaign in Iraq.

Carl Cannon, writing in the *National Journal*, examined surveys of public opinion during these earlier conflicts. When people were asked in 1951 whether the war in Korea was "a mistake," 43 percent of Democrats and 55 percent of Republicans said it was. Note that even though U.S. involvement in the war was the product of a Democratic president, Democratic opposition among those polled was only twelve percentage points less than that of Republicans.

This modest gap did not exist because of elite unity. On the contrary, Democratic and Republican members of Congress were deeply divided. Many congressional Republicans blamed the Democrats for the "loss" of China to Mao Zedong. Senator William Jenner (R-Ind.) called George Marshall, the secretary of defense, a "front man for traitors" and "a living lie." Senator Joseph McCarthy (R-Wis.) called Marshall "completely incompetent" and published a book in which he accused Marshall of being part of a "conspiracy so immense and an infamy so black as to dwarf any previous such venture in the history of man." Senator Richard Nixon (R-Calif.) called for Truman's impeachment. After Truman fired General Douglas MacArthur, the general received the biggest ticker tape parade in the history of New York City; he then gave an emotional defense of himself to a joint session of Congress, leading the Senate Republican Policy Committee to vote unanimously for a manifesto indicting Truman, Marshall, and Secretary of State Dean Acheson for a "super-Munich in Asia." Yet despite all of this, more than a third of all Republican voters (and 40 percent of independents) told pollsters that the war in Korea was not a mistake.

Elite opinion was similarly divided over the war in Vietnam. Senator J. William Fulbright (D-Ark.), chairman of the Foreign Relations Committee, held hearings featuring witnesses who denounced U.S. efforts in Vietnam. Reporting from young journalists who covered the war there was overwhelmingly negative. But when Americans were polled after the Tet Offensive, one third of Republicans, Democrats, and independents said the war "was not a mistake." Political party affiliation made no difference in their perceptions.

Now we come to Iraq. Elite opinion has been divided about this war as well, but now elite divisions are almost precisely mirrored in divisions among the general public. In February 2006, a CBS News poll asked Americans whether the United States "did the right thing in taking military action against Iraq or should the U.S. have stayed out." Among Democrats, 76 percent said the United States should have stayed out; only 25 percent of Republicans said that. (Independent voters were split down the middle.) This is a stark contrast with public opinion during the Vietnam era, when Democrats and Republicans held roughly similar views of the war until well after the Tet Offensive (and even then their views differed only slightly). During the Iraq War, Democrats and Republicans differed from the outset, with the gap widening as the war went on.

Something, then, has changed. Both the Korean and Vietnam wars were controversial, and each was an important element in a presidential campaign (Korea in 1952, Vietnam in 1972). But unlike the situation today with regard to the Iraq War, Democrats and Republicans were not then almost entirely on opposite sides. And the current split over the war is mirrored in many other aspects of foreign and military policy. Republicans, for instance, believe military strength is more important than diplomacy in advancing U.S. interests; Democrats have the opposite view. Republicans define America's international obligations as resisting nuclear proliferation and opposing terrorism; Democrats define it as bringing troops home, fighting AIDS, and improving relations with U.S. allies. If the overseas mission of the United States is defined as expanding democracy, Republicans favor it and Democrats oppose it; if it is defined as enhancing human rights, Democrats support it and Republicans question it.[1]

Why Is Polarization Growing?

Polarization, then, is real. But what explains its growth? And has it spread beyond the political elites to influence the opinions and attitudes of ordinary Americans? The answer to the first question, at least, can be found in the changing politics of Congress, the new competitiveness of the mass media, and the rise of new interest groups.

That Congress is polarized seems beyond question. When, in 1998, the House deliberated whether to impeach President Clinton, all but four Republican members voted for at least one of the impeachment articles, while only five Democrats voted for even one. In the Senate, 91 percent of Republicans voted to convict on at least one article; every single Democrat voted for acquittal.

The impeachment issue was not an isolated case. In 1993, President Clinton's budget passed both the House and the Senate without a single Republican vote in favor. The same deep partisan split occurred over taxes and supplemental appropriations. Nor was this experience under Clinton a blip: since 1950, there has been a steady increase in the percentage of votes in Congress pitting most Democrats against most Republicans.

The reasons for the widening fissures in Congress are not hard to find. Each of the political parties was once a coalition of dissimilar forces: liberal northern Democrats and conservative southern Democrats, liberal coastal Republicans and conservative midwestern Republicans. No longer; the realignments of the South (now overwhelmingly Republican) and of New England (now strongly Democratic) have all but eliminated legislators who deviate from the party's leadership. Conservative Democrats and liberal Republicans are endangered species now approaching extinction. At the same time, the ideological gap between the parties is growing: if there was once a large overlap between Democrats and Republicans—remember "Tweedledum and Tweedledee"?—today that congruence has almost disappeared. By the late 1990s, virtually every Democrat was more liberal than virtually every Republican.

The result has been not only intense partisanship but a sharp rise in congressional incivility. In 1995, a Republican-controlled Senate passed a budget that President Clinton proceeded to veto; in the loggerhead that followed, many federal agencies shut down (in a move that backfired on the Republicans). Congressional debates have seen an increase not only in heated exchanges but in the number of times a representative's words are either ruled out of order or "taken down" (that is, written by the clerk and then read aloud, with the offending member being asked if he or she wishes to withdraw them).

It has been suggested that congressional polarization is exacerbated by new districting arrangements that make each House seat safe for either a Democratic or a Republican incumbent. If only these seats were truly competitive, it is said, more centrist legislators would be elected. That seems plausible, but David C. King of Harvard has shown that it is wrong: in the

House, the more competitive the district, the more extreme the views of the winner. This odd finding is apparently the consequence of a nomination process dominated by party activists. In primary races, where turnout is low (and seems to be getting lower), the ideologically motivated tend to exercise a preponderance of influence.

All this suggests a situation very unlike the half century before the 1990s, though perhaps closer to certain periods in the nineteenth century. Then, too, incivility was common in Congress, with members not only passing the most scandalous remarks about each other but on occasion striking their rivals with canes or fists. Such partisan feeling ran highest when Congress was deeply divided over slavery before the Civil War and over Reconstruction after it. Today the issues are different, but the emotions are not dissimilar.

Next, the role of the mass media in America's growing polarization. Not only are they themselves increasingly polarized, but consumers are well aware of it and act on that awareness. Fewer people now subscribe to newspapers or watch the network evening news. Although some of this decline may be explained by a preference for entertainment over news, some undoubtedly reflects the growing conviction that the mainstream press generally does not tell the truth, or at least not the whole truth.

In part, media bias feeds into, and off, an increase in business competition. In the 1950s, television news amounted to a brief thirty-minute interlude in the day's programming, and not a very profitable one at that; for the rest of the time, the three networks supplied us with westerns and situation comedies. Today, television news is a vast, growing, and very profitable venture by the many broadcast and cable outlets that supply news twenty-four hours a day, seven days a week.

The news we get is not only more omnipresent, it is also more competitive and hence often more adversarial. When there were only three television networks, and radio stations were forbidden by the fairness doctrine from broadcasting controversial views, the media gravitated toward the middle of the ideological spectrum, where the large markets could be found. But now that technology has created cable news and the Internet, and now that the fairness doctrine has by and large been repealed, many media outlets find their markets at the ideological extremes.

Here is where the sharper antagonism among political leaders and their advisers and associates comes in. As one journalist has remarked about the

change in his profession, "We don't deal in facts [any longer], but in attrib-
uted opinions." Or, these days, in unattributed opinions. And those opinions
are more intensely rivalrous than was once the case.

The result is that, through commercial as well as ideological self-interest,
the media contribute heavily to polarization. Broadcasters are eager for stories
to fill their round-the-clock schedules, and at the same time reluctant to trust
the government as a source for those stories. Many media outlets are clearly
liberal in their orientation; with the arrival of Fox News and the growth of talk
radio, many are now just as clearly conservative.

The evidence of liberal bias in the mainstream media is very strong. The
Center for Media and Public Affairs (CMPA) has been systematically studying
television broadcasts for a quarter century. In the 2004 presidential campaign,
John Kerry received more favorable mentions than any presidential candidate
in CMPA's history, especially during the month before election day. This bias
is not new: since 1980 (and setting aside the recent advent of Fox News), the
Democratic candidate has received more favorable mentions than the
Republican candidate in every race except the 1988 contest between Michael
Dukakis and George H. W. Bush. A similarly clear orientation characterizes
weekly newsmagazines like *Time* and *Newsweek*.

For its part, talk radio is listened to by about one-sixth of the adult
public, and that one-sixth is made up mostly of conservatives.[2] On cable-
television news, there is an intense rivalry between CNN and Fox News.
Those who watch CNN are more likely to be Democrats than Republicans;
the reverse is emphatically true of Fox. As for news on the Internet, which has
become an important source for college graduates in particular, it, too, is
largely polarized along political and ideological lines, especially where news
blogs are concerned.

At one time, our culture was only weakly affected by the media because
news organizations had just a few points of access to us and were largely
moderate and audience-maximizing enterprises. Today the media have many
lines of access, and reflect both the maximization of controversy and the
cultivation of niche markets. Once the media talked to us; now they shout
at us.

And then there are the interest groups. In the past, the major ones—the
National Association of Manufacturers, the Chamber of Commerce, and labor
organizations like the AFL-CIO—were concerned with their own material

interests. They are still active, but the loudest messages today come from very different sources and have a very different cast to them. They are issued by groups concerned with social and cultural matters like civil rights, the environment, alternatives to the public schools, the role of women, access to firearms, and so forth, and they directly influence the way people view politics.

Interest groups preoccupied with material concerns can readily find ways to arrive at compromise solutions to their differences; interest groups divided by issues of rights or morality find compromise very difficult. The positions taken by many of these groups and their supporters, often operating within the two political parties, profoundly affect the selection of candidates for office. In brief, it is hard to imagine someone opposed to abortion receiving the Democratic nomination for President, or someone in favor of it receiving the Republican nomination.

Outside the realm of party politics, interest groups also file briefs in important court cases and can benefit from decisions that in turn help shape the political debate. Abortion became a hot controversy in the 1970s not because the American people were already polarized on the matter but because their (mainly centrist) views were not consulted; instead, national policy was determined by the Supreme Court in a decision, *Roe v. Wade*, that itself reflected a definition of "rights" vigorously promoted by certain well-defined interest groups.

Divisions among Ordinary Americans

Polarization not only is real and has increased, but it has also spread to rank-and-file voters through elite influence. In *The Nature and Origins of Mass Opinion* (1992), John R. Zaller of UCLA listed a number of contemporary issues—homosexuality, a nuclear freeze, the war in Vietnam, busing for school integration, the 1990–1991 war to expel Iraq from Kuwait—and measured the views held about them by politically aware citizens. (By "politically aware," Zaller meant people who did well answering neutral factual questions about politics.) His findings were illuminating.

Take the Persian Gulf War. Iraq had invaded Kuwait in August 1990. From that point through the congressional elections in November 1990, scarcely any elite voices were raised to warn against anything the United States might contemplate doing in response. Two days after the mid-term elections, however, President George H. W. Bush announced that he was sending many more troops to the Persian Gulf. This provoked strong criticism from some members of Congress, especially Democrats.

As it happens, a major public opinion survey was under way just as these events were unfolding. Before criticism began to be voiced in Congress, both registered Democrats and registered Republicans had supported Bush's vaguely announced intention of coming to the aid of Kuwait; the more politically aware they were, the greater their support. *After* the onset of elite criticism, the support of Republican voters went up, but Democratic support flattened out. As Bush became more vigorous in enunciating his aims, politically aware voters began to differ sharply, with Democratic support declining and Republican support increasing further.

Much the same pattern can be seen in popular attitudes toward the other issues studied by Zaller. As political awareness increases, attitudes split apart, with, for example, highly aware liberals favoring busing and job guarantees and opposing the war in Vietnam, and highly aware conservatives opposing busing and job guarantees and supporting the war in Vietnam.[3]

But why should this be surprising? To imagine that extremist politics has been confined to the chattering classes is to believe that Congress, the media, and American interest groups operate in an ideological vacuum. I find that assumption implausible.

As for the extent to which these extremist views have spread, that is probably best assessed by looking not at specific issues but at enduring political values and party preferences. In 2004, only 12 percent of Democrats approved of George Bush; at earlier periods, by contrast, three to four times as many Democrats approved of Ronald Reagan, Gerald Ford, Richard Nixon, and Dwight D. Eisenhower. Over the course of about two decades, in other words, party affiliation had come to exercise a critical influence over what people thought about a sitting president.

The same change can be seen in the public's view of military power. Since the late 1980s, Republicans have been more willing than Democrats to say that "the best way to ensure peace is through military strength." By the late 1990s and on into 2003, well over two-thirds of all Republicans agreed with this view, but far fewer than half of all Democrats did. In 2005, three-fourths of all Democrats but fewer than a third of all Republicans told pollsters that good diplomacy was the best way to ensure peace. In the same survey, two-thirds of all Republicans but only one-fourth of all Democrats said they would fight for this country "whether it is right or wrong."

The parties are no longer seen as Tweedledum and Tweedledee. To the contrary, as the parties sharpen *their* ideological differences, attentive voters have sharpened their ideological differences. They now like either the Democrats or the Republicans more than they once did, and are less apt to feel neutral toward either one.

How deep does this polarization reach? As measured by opinion polls, the gap between Democrats and Republicans was twice as great in 2004 as in 1972. In fact, rank-and-file Americans disagree more strongly today than did politically active Americans in 1972.

To be sure, this mass polarization involves only a minority of all voters, but the minority is sizable, and a significant part of it is made up of the college educated. As Marc Hetherington of Vanderbilt puts it: "People with the greatest ability to assimilate new information, those with more formal education, are most affected by elite polarization." And that cohort has undeniably grown.

In 1900, only 10 percent of all young Americans went to high school. My father, in common with many men his age in the early twentieth century, dropped out of school after the eighth grade. Even when I graduated from college, the first in my family to do so, fewer than one-tenth of all Americans over the age of twenty-five had gone that far. Today, 84 percent of adult Americans have graduated from high school and nearly 27 percent have graduated from college. This extraordinary growth in schooling has produced an ever larger audience for political agitation.

Ideologically, an even greater dividing line than undergraduate education is postgraduate education. People who have proceeded beyond college seem to be very different from those who stop with a high-school or college diploma. Thus, about a sixth of all voters describe themselves as liberals, but the figure for those with a postgraduate degree is well over a quarter. In mid-2004, about half of all voters trusted George Bush; less than a third of those with a postgraduate education did. In November of the same year, when over half of all college graduates voted for Bush, well over half of the smaller cohort who had done postgraduate work voted for Kerry. According to the Pew Center for Research on the People and the Press, more than half of all Democrats with a postgraduate education supported the antiwar candidacy of Howard Dean.

The effect of postgraduate education is reinforced by being in a profession. Between 1900 and 1960, write John B. Judis and Ruy Teixeira in *The Emerging Democratic Majority* (2002), professionals voted pretty much the same way as business managers; by 1988, the former began supporting Democrats while the latter supported Republicans. On the other hand, the effect of postgraduate education seems to outweigh the effect of affluence. For most voters, including college graduates, having higher incomes means becoming more conservative; not so for those with a postgraduate education, whose liberal predilections are immune to the wealth effect.

The results of this linkage between ideology, on the one hand, and congressional polarization, media influence, interest-group demands, and education on the other are easily read in the commentary surrounding the 2004 election. In their zeal to denigrate the president, liberals had "gone quite around the twist," in the words of one conservative pundit. According to liberal spokesmen, conservatives with their "religious intolerance" and their determination to rewrite the Constitution had so befuddled their fellow Americans that a "great nation was felled by a poisonous nut."

If such wholesale slurs are not signs of polarization, then the word has no meaning. To a degree that we cannot precisely measure, and over issues that we cannot exactly list, polarization has seeped down into the public, where it has assumed the form of a culture war. The sociologist James Davison Hunter, who has written about this phenomenon in a mainly religious context, defines culture war as "political and social hostility rooted in different systems of moral understanding." Such conflicts, he writes, which can involve "fundamental ideas about who we are as Americans," are waged both across the religious/secular divide and within religions themselves, where those with an "orthodox" view of moral authority square off against those with a "progressive" view.

To some degree, this terminology is appropriate to today's political situation as well. We are indeed in a culture war in Hunter's sense, though I believe this war is itself but another component, or another symptom, of the larger ideological polarization that has us in its grip. Conservative thinking on political issues has religious roots, but it also has roots that are fully as secular as anything on the Left. By the same token, the liberal attack on conservatives derives in part from an explicitly "progressive" religious orientation—liberal Protestantism or Catholicism, or Reform Judaism—but also in part from the same secular sources shared by many conservatives.

What's Wrong with Polarization?

But what, one might ask, is wrong with having well-defined parties arguing vigorously about the issues that matter? Is it possible that polarized politics is a good thing, encouraging sharp debate and clear positions? Perhaps that is true on those issues where reasonable compromises can be devised. But there are two limits to such an arrangement.

First, many Americans believe that unbridgeable political differences have prevented leaders from addressing the problems they were elected to address. As a result, distrust of government mounts, leading to an alienation from politics altogether. The steep decline in popular approval of our national officials has many causes, but surely one of them is that ordinary voters agree among themselves more than political elites agree with each other—and the elites are far more numerous than they once were.

In the 1950s, a committee of the American Political Science Association (APSA) argued the case for a "responsible" two-party system. The model the APSA had in mind was the more ideological and therefore more "coherent" party system of Great Britain. At the time, scarcely anyone thought our parties could be transformed in such a supposedly salutary direction. Instead, as Governor George Wallace of Alabama put it in his failed third-party bid for the presidency, there was not a "dime's worth of difference" between Democrats and Republicans.

What Wallace forgot was that, however alike the parties were, the public liked them that way. A half-century ago, Tweedledum and Tweedledee enjoyed the support of the American people; the more different they have become, the greater has been the drop in popular confidence in both them and the federal government.

A final drawback of polarization is more profound. Sharpened debate is arguably helpful with respect to domestic issues, but not for the management of important foreign and military matters. The United States, an unrivaled superpower with unparalleled responsibilities for protecting the peace and defeating terrorists, is now forced to discharge those duties with its own political house in disarray.

We fought World War II as a united nation, even against two enemies (Germany and Italy) that had not attacked us. We began the wars in Korea and Vietnam with some degree of unity, too, although it was eventually whittled away. By the early 1990s, when we expelled Iraq from Kuwait, we had to do so over the objections of congressional critics; the first President Bush avoided putting the issue to Congress altogether. In 2003 we toppled Saddam Hussein in the face of catcalls from many domestic leaders and opinion makers. Now, in stabilizing Iraq and helping that country create a new free government, we have proceeded despite intense and mounting criticism, much of it voiced by politicians who before the war agreed that Saddam Hussein was an evil menace in possession of weapons of mass destruction and that we had to remove him.

Denmark or Luxembourg can afford to exhibit domestic anguish and uncertainty over military policy; the United States cannot. A divided America encourages our enemies, disheartens our allies, and saps our resolve—potentially to fatal effect. What General Giap of North Vietnam once said of us is even truer today: America cannot be defeated on the battlefield, but it can be defeated at home. Polarization is a force that can defeat us.

Notes

1. The preceding five paragraphs are from my essay in Pietro S. Nivola and David W. Brady, eds., *Red and Blue Nation? Consequences and Correction of America's Polarized Politics*, vol. 2. (Washington, D.C.: Brookings Institution, 2008), 168–72.

2. The political disposition of most radio talk-show hosts is explained by William G. Mayer in "Why Talk Radio Is Conservative," *Public Interest*, Summer 2004.

3. True, the "elite effect" may not be felt across the board. With most of the issues Zaller investigated, even well-informed citizens would have had little first-hand experience, and so their minds were of necessity open to the influence of their "betters." Results might have been different had he measured their views on matters about which most Americans believe themselves to be personally well informed: crime, inflation, drug abuse, or their local schools.

PART II

Religion and Politics

8

Religion and Polarization

Originally published in America at Risk: Threats to Liberal Self-Government in an Age of Uncertainty, *ed. Robert Faulkner and Susan Shell, University of Michigan Press, 2009*

America is the most religious of all industrialized democracies, a fact that has important political consequences. Though the number of atheists and agnostics has grown, religion plays an important role in what people believe and how they vote.

Religion may be one of the most important sources of polarization in American politics. Though deep political divisions occur among both religious and secular people, the split between the religious and the secular is large and has grown. In 2004, white voters who attend religious services at least weekly were three times as likely as those who seldom or never went to church to oppose abortion and twice as likely to object to gay marriage and to describe themselves as conservative. Among whites, religious identification is more closely associated with the presidential vote than is age, sex, income, or education.[1]

The importance of religion was emphasized by editorial comment after the 2004 election. A series of angry statements accused President Bush of having led a "jihad" against the American people by attempting to found a "theocratic" state in which "Christian fundamentalists" would use their "religious energy to promote divisions and intolerance at home and abroad."[2] Pundits eagerly looked for evidence that the election was settled by voters who had embraced "moral values," presumably the wrong ones.

Following the election we heard another round of disagreements involving religious belief. Many defenders of Terri Schiavo accused those who wished to let her die of being godless murderers; many who supported the withdrawal of her feeding tubes charged that her supporters were radical fundamentalists who sought a theocratic state.[3]

The Historical Legacy of Religion

Religion has always played an important role in American culture and has at times been the source of deep political divisions. One does not have to be a close student of American history to recall that religion has animated both worrisome and worthy causes. Religious differences animated the objections of the Know Nothing party to the presence of American Catholics but it also supplied the moral outrage against the ownership of human beings. The civil rights movement was led by the Rev. Martin Luther King, Jr., and his appeal was essentially religious in nature. Southern white Protestant churches, though they had long been a part of a segregated society, did not resist King's claims. Though many churches were passive or silent, some, such as the Southern Baptists and Southern Presbyterians, publicly supported desegregation.[4] And those who opposed the war in Vietnam rarely, if ever, complained that the Rev. William Sloane Coffin appealed to God to argue against American involvement there.[5]

Historian David Chappell has argued that many leaders of American liberalism during the 1940s and 1950s worried that their cause, based on a reasoned commitment to social improvement, was in danger of languishing because it lacked a moral fervor sufficient to keep intact a coalition of blacks, union workers, big-city bosses, southern whites, and northern intellectuals. The New Deal coalition, he argues, consisted of "hungry liberals" who sensed that "something was missing."[6] John Dewey, in the 1920s, argued that liberalism needed a "religious belief" that was devoid of any connection to actual religions. That belief was important, he wrote, because "liberals are notoriously hard to organize," whereas conservatives had a "natural bond of cohesion based on habit, tradition, and fear of the unknown."[7] Dewey never made quite clear just exactly how one creates a religious belief without being religious.

Later, Lionel Trilling took up the same argument. When he wrote in the early 1950s, liberalism was, he said, "the sole intellectual tradition in

American politics," but that tradition, important as it is, was trying to organize the world in a rational way, thereby leading it to drift "toward a denial of the emotions and the imagination."[8]

The civil rights movement put a brief end to these worries because religion helped galvanize the most important social movement of the twentieth century. And when Jimmy Carter ran for the presidency in 1976 he brought to his candidacy the support of many evangelicals. In that year, only about one-third of all self-identified white evangelicals described themselves as Republicans (even though about half voted for Gerald Ford). Carter, and then Clinton after him, carried several southern states with evangelical help. By 1996, however, matters had changed. By then, white Protestant evangelicals had become much more conservative, more Republican in party identification, and more likely to vote for the Republican presidential candidate. In 1976 these voters made up only one-sixth of all Republican supporters; by 1996, they made up one-third of that support.[9]

Religion and Public Opinion

One interpretation of the current furor over religion in American politics is that secular liberals embrace religion when it supports civil rights and gives aid to Democratic candidates and denounce it when it opposes abortion and backs Republican candidates. But this view is uncharitable because there are many religious liberals just as there are many nonreligious conservatives; the votes of each group often depend on matters having little to do with faith.

Americans are divided in their religious activities. Though the great majority believe in God and life after death, secularists (by which I mean people in whose lives religion plays no role whether or not they believe in God or an afterlife) are rising in number. They tend to live in big cities on the Pacific Coast or in the Northeast and are likely to have voted for Al Gore in 2000 and for John F. Kerry in 2004.[10] Religion is not a trivial factor in presidential elections. America's secular voters tend to live in blue counties whereas America's religious ones live in red ones.

In 2004, nearly two-thirds of the people who said they attended church more than weekly voted for Bush and only one-third voted for Kerry. But these voters make up only one-sixth of the electorate. Of the voters who said they never attend church, two-thirds voted for Kerry and only one-third for Bush, but these voters make up only one-seventh of the electorate. And between 2000 and 2004 Bush gained support among people who said they attended church rarely or never. In short, religion makes a difference, but very religious and very irreligious voters are only a minority of the electorate. And the number of voters who considered moral values (whatever that may mean) the most important issue for them was lower in 2004 than it had been in 1996 and 2000. In 2004 terrorism and Iraq were the most important issues to most people. People who were concerned about terrorism mostly voted for Bush; those concerned about Iraq mostly voted for Kerry. And the former outnumbered the latter.[11]

Traditional evangelical Protestants made up over one-fourth of all the voters who supported Bush. If you add to that share the votes of traditionalist Catholics and Protestants and other evangelicals, you account for over one-half of his vote. Atheists, agnostics, and secularists made up one-sixth of all of the supporters of Kerry, and if you add to that the votes of Jews and black Protestants, you get almost half of Kerry's vote. Between 2000 and 2004, Bush gained support among traditional religious groups while the Democratic candidate gained support among modernist religious groups, atheists, and agnostics.[12]

Religion Abroad

Religion makes a difference here and helps explain the polarization of the American electorate. This is in sharp contrast to Europe, where religion has almost ceased to have any cultural or political role at all, especially in the north. In 1998, the proportion of people attending religious services once a week or more often was 5 percent in France and 4 percent in England and Denmark, and it was comparably low in other Protestant nations. Even in Catholic Italy and Spain, no more than a third of all adults frequently attended church. Only in Ireland is church attendance high, involving about two-thirds of the people.[13] After the Second World War, religious affiliation was probably more important than social class in explaining why French and German voters supported either Catholic or Socialist parties, but by the 1980s politics in Europe had lost most of its religious basis.[14] In the

United States, by contrast, frequent attendance at religious services is about the same today as it was in 1981, and involves, by some contested estimates, nearly half the population.[15] Moreover, a much higher percentage of Americans pray than do any Europeans except, again, the Irish.[16]

Though there has been a growth in the proportion of nonreligious or secular voters in the United States, that growth is nothing like what has occurred in most of Europe. This difference requires one to address the secularization theory. As originally stated, it argues that modernization, by which is meant the growth of rational and instrumental inquiry, leads to a decline in the social significance of religion. Modernization means the growth of institutions that manage education and welfare, a decline in the fraction of people living in small communities, and a sharp increase in scientific thought. These forces, as John Stuart Mill, Karl Marx, August Comte, Emile Durkheim, Max Weber, and many others have argued, lead to a subordination of religious thought. If factories teach technical skills, if public schools provide nondenominational education, if health and welfare agencies care for the sick and the deprived, if people live mixed together in large cities that display the benefits of a consumer society, and if science seeks only naturalistic explanations for everything from the nature of life to the origins of the cosmos, what can religion possibly offer?

But almost all of the world is modernized or modernizing, and religious belief, outside of Europe, seems hardly to have diminished. And the United States, perhaps the most modern society in the world, is filled with people who believe in God, go to church or synagogue, and pray to the Almighty. The secularization theory may be in some trouble. And not only in the United States. There has been a rapid growth in Protestant religions in Latin America, the Caribbean, Asia, and Africa. Comprehensive data comparing countries outside of Europe and North America are lacking, but the best available evidence suggests that there has been a rapid growth in Protestant, and especially Pentecostal, churches in much of the world. In Brazil there are more Protestant pastors than Catholic priests. There has been similar growth in Chile and Guatemala. In South Korea the number of Protestant churches is increasing five times faster than the Korean population.[17]

That modernity need not spell the end of religion is certainly the view of Professor Peter Berger, who has recanted his earlier view that modernity would produce secular societies.[18] According to him and to some other scholars, we are seeing as much growth as decline in religion around the world, and much of this growth is occurring, not in old villages, but in big cities, and not simply in developing nations such as Guatemala but in industrialized ones such as South Korea.

There are two views one can take on this matter. One is that America is the exceptional state, modern without being secular, whereas Europe shows the powerfully secular effects of modernization. The other is that Europe is the exception, since America and much of Asia are responding to modernity without abandoning religion.

To me, the most interesting question is why America is more religious than Europe, and especially England. After all, England settled the American colonies with people who were, in most cases, deeply religious. Both countries were among the first to practice representative government and both celebrated individual rights; indeed, as I and others have argued elsewhere, England invented individualism.[19] Despite individualism, religious activities were alike in both countries up to about a hundred years ago. Scholars have estimated that in the second half of the nineteenth century, about half the adult population in England was in church on Sunday, and something like that fraction in the United States.[20] In 1860, one-fifth of all of the adult males in New York City served on the boards of Protestant organizations, and about half of all adult Protestant males were members of at least one church-related voluntary association.[21] In the late 1820s over 40 percent of young children in New York City and about half of those in England attended Sunday schools.[22]

America and England were alike in the nineteenth century but by the middle of the twentieth had become completely different. America continued to be a nation of churchgoers while England stopped being one. Today half of American adults go to church but less than one-twentieth of English adults do.[23]

The Persistence of Religion in America

There is no single or simple explanation for America and England becoming so religiously different. One possibility is that America was settled by millions of immigrants who brought their religion with them,[24] but that can be only part of the story. Churchgoing is especially strong today in counties with relatively few immigrants. Moreover, the great increase in American religiosity occurred long before the Irish and Italians arrived in large numbers. Professors Rodney Stark and Roger Finke, reanalyzing data first published in the 1930s, estimate that there was a dramatic growth in church congregations and membership between 1776 and 1850, long before European Catholics began arriving, and that the largest increases were among Baptists and Methodists.[25] The increase in membership continued right into the 1980s (except for a brief decline during the Civil War years). In addition, the rapid growth in the number of Mormons, a faith that, at least in America, has not emphasized recruitment among immigrants, suggests that immigration cannot be the entire explanation for American religiosity.[26]

It is striking that German immigrants arriving in America were like Germans still living in their homeland: that is, most were Lutherans who did not go to church frequently. But third-generation Germans here are much like Americans: that is, they have joined the Baptist, Methodist, or some evangelical church and attend services as frequently as most Americans.[27]

A second explanation that also has some importance is one advanced by Professor Jose Casanova: Europe was governed by "caesaropapist churches," while America was not.[28] If I may translate from Casanova's sociological jargon, I believe he means that Europe was for centuries ruled by nations or principalities that combined church and state into an absolutist rule (though after the Protestant Reformation it seems a bit misleading to call Calvin's Geneva or Luther's Sweden "papist").

His central argument, if not his language, is, I believe, correct. Where the state enforced religious orthodoxy, both the church and the state were vulnerable to popular revolts. The hostility to liberalism expressed by Pope Pius IX meant that European states had to choose between obedience and rebellion. Sometimes, as with the *Kulturkampf* in Germany in the nineteenth century, the state attacked the status of the Catholic Church. The demand for representative government was inevitably linked to the demand for religious freedom. One could not endorse the French Revolution without attacking the Catholic Church that had for decades been protected by the state. And even when the church lost its monopoly power, many European states continued to participate in its management in ways that made political dissent equivalent to religious dissent. In France, the state must still approve the appointment of Catholic bishops.[29] In Scandinavia, where the official churches are Protestant, these religious bodies were not disestablished so much as converted into instruments of the welfare state. In Sweden, the government supports a state church with tax revenues; church laws are passed by parliament and all bishops are appointed by the state. At the same time, Sweden has abolished all religious requirements for serving on church governing boards, a step that has allowed church control to be placed in the hands of atheists. In virtually every European nation, there is a tax-supported state church.[30]

When this is the case, political and religious affiliations tend to coincide. In much of Europe, Catholic political parties arose after the First World War; in countries such as Belgium, Germany, Italy, and the Netherlands these parties governed the country for many years. Religiously defined parties helped bring voters into representative government, but rule by Christian Democrats did nothing to strengthen Christianity. On the contrary, people who opposed Christian parties learned to oppose Christianity. A liberal or socialist party (or in France, a Gaullist one) became almost by definition a non-Christian one.[31]

Tocqueville explained the advantages of a separation of church and state in 1835: In nations where religion forms "an alliance with a political power, religion augments its authority over a few and forfeits the hope of reigning over all." When this alliance exists, as it has in Europe, the "unbelievers of Europe attack the Christians as their political opponents rather than as their religious adversaries."[32]

England, like the countries of Europe, has had a state church. For centuries Catholics ruled but then were replaced by Anglicans; for a brief period the Puritans ruled. Beginning in the latter part of the seventeenth century, officeholders had to subscribe to Anglicanism, and students matriculating at Oxford and Cambridge had to sign the Thirty-Nine Articles of Anglican faith. Marriages and burials had to follow Anglican rites. When a liberal political movement emerged in the nineteenth century, nonconformist sects were part of its animating spirit; as William Gladstone said, nonconformity was the "backbone" of the English Liberal Party.[33] The efforts by Anabaptists, Catholics, Jews, Methodists, Quakers, and Unitarians to carve out religious freedom were, of necessity, focused on the state and its traditional religious authority.

Religion, Politics, and Markets

The close ties between state and church have no counterpart in the United States. It is true, of course, that many colonies in America had important religious policies. Six required their voters to be Protestants, four said their citizens must believe in the divine inspiration of the Bible, one required belief in the Trinity and two in heaven and hell, and five had an officially established church.[34] But the United States could be created out of these colonies only by adopting a federal Constitution that left all of these matters to the states. The Constitution said nothing about religion except to ban religious tests for office, and the First Amendment made it impossible ever to have a national church. (Just what else the Amendment means by its ban on any law "respecting an establishment of religion" is unclear, but that it banned a national religion or church is indisputable.)

The reason for official national silence on religious matters owes something to the writings of John Locke, Roger Williams, James Madison, and other defenders of religious tolerance, but it owes even more, I think, to the fact that no national union was possible if the federal government had any religious powers. Americans were worried that a national government with religious powers would persecute dissenters here just as they had been attacked in England. Religion was felt to be a state matter, and remained so until the Supreme Court changed the rules in 1947.[35]

Though the newly united American states took religion seriously, the people did not define themselves by their religious or ethnic identity, but by the American Creed as set forth in the Declaration of Independence.

Despite federal silence on religious matters, in America there have been many political movements linked to religious ideas. Indeed, the nation became, as Mark DeWolfe Howe put it, a de facto Protestant state, with local schools teaching religious beliefs, state governments enforcing the Sabbath with blue laws, and many political efforts to mobilize anti-Catholic sentiment. In Oregon, the Ku Klux Klan and other groups obtained passage of a law that banned Catholics from running their own schools, a policy that was struck down by a unanimous Supreme Court.[36]

One of the reasons that a policy of separating church and state found so many Protestant supporters was its tendency to prevent the Roman Catholic church from unifying church and state. Preventing such a unification was the goal of many Protestant demands, some based on describing the Pope as the Antichrist and including the demand for the passage of the Blaine Amendment in 1874. The amendment was never ratified, but copies of it found their way into several state constitutions.

There was, of course, never much evidence that Catholics wanted to merge state and church. Indeed, Protestant demands that public schools teach Protestantism led many Catholic leaders to endorse the principle of separation and favor locally controlled school districts as ways of preventing anti-Catholic programs.[37] In short, in a religiously diverse nation, pressure came from several religions to avoid state influence on churches.

Despite the many state efforts to benefit or attack religion, the absence of any federal policy on the matter has made America fundamentally different from England. American churches find themselves in a free market where their existence and growth depend entirely on their own efforts. They get no tax money and confront federal officials who are indifferent to any demands for support. The churches and synagogues that grow are the ones that offer people something of value; the ones that decline are those that offer people relatively little of value except such social status as may come from being seen at services.[38] Privatizing religion has generated religious growth just as privatizing business has encouraged economic development.

In England religion was closely linked both to political authority and to social status. Into the twentieth century, Protestantism was associated with the monarchy and the empire, and religion was linked at first with aristocratic hierarchies and then with radical theologians, neither of whom earned much respect from the average Briton. Even today, the Archbishop of Canterbury is appointed by the prime minister. In England the Anglican Church offered aristocratic bravado and then Christian Socialism, later renamed Christian Sociology.[39] England had no local governments or local units of political parties that could be controlled by religious groups, and scarcely any local media that could represent religious preferences. Methodism in England began as a dissenting group among Anglicans; for many years Methodists sought to maintain their status as an especially devout but not rebellious part of the Church of England, and so surrendered much of their evangelical zeal.[40]

The contrast with America could not be sharper. Dean M. Kelley, a member of the liberal National Council of Churches, has observed the growth of religiously demanding churches and the decline of religiously undemanding ones. What we now call the mainline Protestant churches—the Episcopalians, Methodists, Presbyterians, and the more theologically liberal Lutheran churches—are losing members, while the more ardent, evangelical, and fundamentalist churches—the Southern Baptists, Mormons, Seventh Day Adventists, Jehovah's Witnesses, Assemblies of God, and the Salvation Army—are growing in membership.[41] This difference arises not because mainline churches are politically liberal, but because they do not offer a compelling set of religious incentives, namely, finding salvation through Christ, supplying meaningful worship services, and providing religious instruction.[42] The churches that are losing members are, in Kelley's words, "reasonable" and "sociable," while those winning members are "unreasonable and unsociable." They are "unreasonable" in that they refuse to recognize the validity of the teachings of other churches, observe unusual rituals and peculiar dietary customs, practice temperance, and disregard what some people, especially secularists, would call the decent opinions of mankind.

These arguments by a religious leader have been supported by the work of empirical scholars. Laurence Iannacone and his colleagues have shown that strict Protestant churches grow more rapidly than lax ones because strictness raises the level of membership commitment, increases the benefits of belonging, discourages participation in rival organizations, and reduces the number of free riders who go to church but pass on to others the costs of attending. Compared to mainline churches, strict ones grow more rapidly and have higher rates of participation, and these relationships exist independently of members' age, sex, race, income, geographical location, or marital status. These findings help to explain why church growth abroad is most rapid in nations that have no state church.[43]

Matters are more complicated in nations that have dictatorial political regimes, as did the old Soviet Union and many Muslim states today. Where there is political freedom, the absence of a state church facilitates the growth of religion; where political freedom is lacking, state churches may require participation or a secular regime may make public displays of religion undesirable. These are contested issues, and one should compare the work of Iannacone and others who stress markets with that of Pippa Norris and Ronald Inglehart, who emphasize cultural values.[44] In my view, Adam Smith was not only correct about what produces economic prosperity; he was correct about what produces religious success.[45]

The growing churches are trying to provide meaning to life, not simply lectures on political issues and pleasant social affairs, all accompanied by a critical view of the Bible, a generous recognition of individual differences, and the belief that no one has a monopoly on the truth. The growing churches "try to make sense out of experience, even if we have to resort to non-sense to do it."[46] American Methodists never tried to work within the confines of a state church, but from the first established themselves as the leaders of independent camp meetings led by itinerant preachers. Political and cultural localism sustained here what political and cultural centralization curbed in England.

The reason that some churches are growing worries many people who think, rightly, that the churches oppose the Enlightenment and, wrongly, that this opposition leads to bad public policies. I outline my own view below.

Religion Constrained by Politics

One must begin by recognizing that both secular and religious groups can do undesirable or even terrible things. Churches in America have supported blue laws, but secularists have supported the more extreme forms of political correctness. Some religious extremists have murdered abortion workers, but the Weather Underground and the Symbionese Liberation Army, both totally devoid of any religious sentiments, murdered people and blew up buildings. Evangelical and fundamentalist religions have opposed abortion and rejected homosexual marriage, but secular courts have created this conflict by authorizing abortions and homosexual marriage without any democratic support. Religious leaders encouraged the Crusades that resulted in looting and death, but fascism and Stalinism killed millions of innocent people. Fanaticism is an equal opportunity employer.

My central argument is that in the United States, unlike in England or Europe, religion has had a remarkably democratic character. Protestant churches organized people on the basis of their consent, involved themselves in cultural but not political conflicts within the state, and acquired status locally because in this country political authority was decentralized. American churches created problems, of course. Protestantism, though democratic, was not always liberal (by "liberal" I mean disposed toward personal freedom). Though it was preoccupied with cultural rather than political issues, Protestantism was often anti-Catholic and sought political power to enforce blue laws. Protestantism, though decentralized, could use local political authority to do unwise things, such as to attack evolutionary biology.

But taken as a whole, rising church movements here were compatible with and even encouraged an open society by supporting personal choice, by not arguing for a state-supported church, and by limiting their actions to local governments rather than trying to manage the nation as a whole.

Religion has, of course, had an impact on American public policy. Because it is powerful in certain localities, it carries weight when it tries to block congressional votes going toward causes it rejects. This is true under both Democratic and Republican administrations, and means that organized religion can provide vetoes much as can Planned Parenthood and the National Rifle Association.

But as with other organizations with strong local constituencies, religion must compete with rival interests to obtain whatever new legislation it wishes. Despite the presence of conservative presidents, scarcely any bill favored by what is now called the Christian Right has been passed by Congress. Protestant leaders could not prevent the creation of Catholic schools, and religious activists could not legally install school prayer, maintain a ban on abortion, or obtain meaningful bans on pornography.[47] Despite the efforts of the Moral Majority and the *700 Club*, conservative religious voters could not nominate a presidential candidate. And several religious leaders have suffered, just as several political ones have, from various scandals.[48] The very factors that encourage religious organizations (free markets, a decentralized government, a localized media) are the same things that discourage religious activists from having much impact on national or even state policy.[49]

In England, by contrast, the alliance between Anglican ministers and political authorities, the need for nonconforming sects to struggle against a state church, and the deep social class basis of religion meant that either religion would be imposed from above or it would vanish for lack of success. As England became more tolerant, no enforced religion could be imposed; but as England remained centralized, religion would lack the "unlimited social space"[50] that it enjoyed in America. And so religion in England collapsed while in America it grew.

The Constraints of Political Life

Christian political activists have responded to this reality by adapting to the constraints of American politics. As a political scientist, I am naturally inclined to look for the constraining effects of culture and constitutions. Even allowing for my bias, I am persuaded that religious leaders, like political and economic ones, adjust to the opportunities and barriers our political and legal system has created.

To reach these conclusions one first has to wade through and then overcome the rhetoric with which Christian political leaders and their critics surround themselves. When Rev. Jerry Falwell founded the Moral Majority in the 1970s, he claimed that it had four million members with two million active donors, and some liberal critics were worried that it was a "disciplined, charging army."[51] In fact, it was neither disciplined nor an army and had vastly fewer members than its leaders proclaimed; by 1987 it had closed down for want of any influence. It was replaced by several organizations, including the Christian Coalition led by Ralph Reed, but the coalition adapted to past failures by moderating religious rhetoric and identifying reasonable goals it could attain by working in parallel with the Republican Party. For example, coalition leaders tried to restrict rather than outlaw abortion and worked toward obtaining a child tax credit. The most extreme religious activists were kept out of leadership posts.[52] In Virginia the Christian Coalition worked with secular conservatives, such as Republican governor George Allen in his 1993 campaign. Allen refused to argue for a ban on abortion, but conservative Christians backed him because they had learned to settle for half a loaf.[53]

Religious activism is constrained in America, as Robert Wuthnow has pointed out, by a culture that has for many decades struggled with the tension between Christianity and civility, the need to cope with political resistance, and the ecumenical efforts of such organizations as the National Conference of Christians and Jews.[54]

The constraints imposed by America's culture and Constitution affected many faiths. During the nineteenth and early twentieth centuries, Roman

Catholicism was under attack here because it was seen as a hierarchical church that had attacked liberalism. But that claim about American Catholics was never true; Alexis de Tocqueville and Harriet Martineau had both pointed out early in the nineteenth century that (in the words of the latter) "the Catholic religion is modified by the spirit of the time in America."[55] Despite this reality, the attacks on Catholics increased, and by 1949 Paul Blanshard's book, *American Freedom and Catholic Power*, was a best seller, warmly endorsed by John Dewey, Lewis Mumford, Reinhold Niebuhr, and Bertrand Russell.[56] They seemingly had good grounds for their concerns: Catholic leaders had endorsed autocracy in Spain and Portugal and the Pope had signed a concordat with Hitler.

But at the very same time, Catholic theologians such as Jacques Maritain in France and John Courtney Murray in this country were modifying Catholic philosophy in order to accommodate it to American sensibilities. They set forth an American Catholic position based on a concern for democracy and individual rights. Their views, however much they may have irritated the Vatican, fit nicely with the actual experience of American Catholics, and, after John F. Kennedy won the presidency in 1960, anti-Catholic sentiment began to evaporate. Catholics behaved in much the same way as conservative Protestants: to persuade Americans, you must be American.

Identifying Religious Voters

Liberal critics of Christian conservatives would have you believe that the Christian Right consists of fundamentalist evangelicals who, lacking much education and living in small southern towns, are conspiring under the direction of their ministers to take over the nation.

To address this argument one must again sort through the rhetoric. First, some distinctions. Fundamentalists are not necessarily (or even often) evangelicals; neither group has origins in the South; their leaders have often been people of considerable education; and the great majority of churchgoers attend services where politics is not mentioned. Fundamentalists believe in the accuracy of the Bible and often work hard to maintain the correctness of their view against other Protestant denominations. Evangelicals may or may not have a fundamentalist view; their mission is less to defend the faith than to recruit new members to it. Both movements were created, not in the South, but in Boston, Chicago, and New York City, and their intellectual sponsorship was at the Princeton Theological Seminary and the Yale Divinity School. Most of the early leaders were affluent and well educated, and on many political issues these groups have either endorsed liberal views or worked in concert with progressive leaders on such matters as restricting immigration.[57] In the 2004 elections, 87 percent of church ministers never mentioned a candidate, and of those who did, the majority did not urge a vote for either candidate.[58]

Fundamentalists and evangelicals were not always allies and on occasion became bitter opponents. Some fundamentalists, having failed to defeat the liberal Social Gospel, turned away from all alliances and often departed their own churches to found new, doctrinally pure ones. Fundamentalists emphasized their rejection of worldly delights, which often meant rejecting the world itself. Evangelicals, on the other hand, were eager to spread the word without abandoning their churches. Such leaders as Charles Fuller and Billy Graham wanted to save souls more than they sought doctrinal purity. When it was founded, the National Association of Evangelicals invited Pentecostals and Anabaptists to join them, much to the horror of fundamentalists. (One early fundamentalist minister called Pentecostals "the last vomit of Satan."[59]) The split between fundamentalists and evangelicals became vivid when, in 1957, Billy Graham asked the liberal Protestant Council of New York City to help organize his crusade.[60]

Analyzing fundamentalists and evangelicals is difficult because public opinion surveys are not very good ways of measuring deep subjective states. As Professor Christian Smith has pointed out, when the Gallup poll defines evangelicals, it asserts that they believe that the Bible is literally true, have had a "born again" experience, and have recruited others to Christianity. But his own detailed interviews show that self-identified evangelicals often differ from these Gallup traits: some doubt that the Bible is literally true, some have not been born again, and some never recruit anyone. If you use the Gallup definition of an evangelical, you discover that they do not have much education. But if you let people define themselves as evangelical, they turn out to be very well educated.[61] Self-identified evangelicals tell pollsters that they are more educated than nonreligious respondents. One-quarter are high school graduates, a fifth are college graduates, and a sixth have done postgraduate work. By contrast, one-fifth of nonreligious people have not even graduated from high school.[62]

Christian evangelicals and fundamentalists are alike in having become conservative. But that statement is not much different from noting that secular voters have become liberal. The Princeton Theological Seminary and the Yale Divinity School may once have encouraged evangelical Christianity, but today they are barely able to endorse Christianity.

If you use the best surveys to compare conservative Protestants to all other Americans, you discover that they differ in some ways and are alike in others. Conservative Protestants, unlike most Americans, believe morality is based on an absolute standard, that religion should play a role in public life, and that salvation can be found only through Jesus Christ. But conservative Protestants are like all other Americans in their support of civil liberties (even for people with whom they disagree), respect for Jews, willingness to let people live by their own morality (even when it is not Christian), and attitudes toward abortion.

The Apparent Benefits of Religion

Religion is also important in a deeper, nonpolitical way. There is a growing body of evidence that suggests that, other things being equal, people with a strong religious faith are more likely to live in two-parent families, achieve upward economic mobility, resist the lures of drugs and crime, overcome health problems, and give money to charity (including to nonreligious charities). I use the word "suggests" very deliberately, for when scholars look at the effects of religion "other things being equal," it is obvious that other things are not entirely equal. After all, people who take religion seriously are likely to differ from those who do not in some important but unmeasured way. We cannot fully control for unmeasured difference by statistical manipulations. It would be nice to assign religious beliefs to a random sample of people and then observe their effects, but happily that is impossible.

Nevertheless, there are many studies that find these religious effects independently of the sex, age, race, and income of people, and so together they create an important argument that ought to be taken seriously.

In 1998 a review of several dozen studies of religion and health concluded that "religious commitment may play a beneficial role in preventing mental and physical illness, improving how people cope with mental and physical illness, and facilitating recovery for illness."[63]

In 1979–1980 a survey was conducted by the National Bureau of Economic Research among black males ages sixteen to twenty-four living in the poorest neighborhoods of Boston, Chicago, and Philadelphia. Religiosity was measured by statements about the strength of religion in the lives of respondents and the frequency of church attendance. Crime was measured by whether respondents said that they had committed any of several illegal acts in the last year. Scholars found an association between religiosity and low levels of delinquency after controlling for other factors, such as age, education, gang membership, or living in public housing or with a single parent.[64] Essentially the same findings emerge from a study that uses a different source of data (black respondents in the National Youth Survey) and takes into account the influence of neighborhood disorder on crime. Crime rates are lower when the respondents attend church frequently, and church attendance tends to immunize people from the hostile effects of disorderly neighborhoods. These effects exist even after controlling for sex, age, single-parent families, and links to deviant peers.[65]

There is also evidence of an association between religious affiliation and the extent to which women cohabit rather than marry; the least religious are more likely to cohabit, the most religious are more likely to marry.[66] Similar findings suggest that suicide, alcoholism, and drug abuse are less common among religious than among nonreligious people,[67] while marital happiness, illegitimacy, and the absence of depression are more common.

Deeply religious people contribute more to charity in this country than do secular people, even after controlling for differences and partisanship. That is, religious liberals and conservatives alike give much more to charity than do their secular counterparts. Moreover, this higher charitable giving among religious people is not confined to religious recipients; religious people give more than secular ones to nonreligious causes.[68]

All of these arguments have to be placed into context. There are many nonreligious people who are healthy and happy, do not abuse alcohol or drugs, are not likely to kill themselves, and are philanthropic to a fault. But among people at risk for these problems because they are poor or live in bad neighborhoods, religion may buffer the otherwise harmful effects of their environment.

This is a hard argument to sustain before an academic audience, because many professors and intellectuals are the creatures of detached reason for whom religion is a sign of personal failure, low self-esteem, or pure ignorance. The chasm of repugnance and dislike that separates Americans who are secular from those who are religious is a great pity. Professor William J. Stuntz of the Harvard Law School—a self-described evangelical Protestant who works at a secular university and who is a red-state voter in a blue state— has fretted in an important essay about how much each side has to learn from the other. Both sides—those in churches and those teaching at universities—struggle to understand difficult texts, worry about important ideas, and share a concern for helping the poor. Instead of recognizing what it shares with the other, each side is preoccupied with abortion and views the other with deep suspicion. Professor Stuntz recounts the remarks of a faculty colleague who said he was the first Christian he had ever met who wasn't stupid, and of a member of his church who thought that being a Christian lawyer was like being a Christian prostitute.[69]

Our Shared Obligations

Both sides could use a bit more humility. Evangelical Christians often forget that it was the Enlightenment and its commitment to scientific learning that helped create a prosperous modern world, while secular professors seem to ignore the unease and uncertainty that necessarily afflicts everyone who wishes to understand the human condition.

Religion has flourished in the United States because the United States is free. Countries that were never free or that retained a state-controlled church are religious in a very different way; it is either underground or radicalized or both. In these countries, either religion, and the deep human yearnings that sustain it, were never allowed to express themselves, or the state has made religion a divisive matter about which the people vote.

As Alan Wolfe has made clear, American democracy has shaped American religion just as much as religion has influenced our democracy. It is easy to overlook this mutual effect. Liberals often wrongly think that what religious people say about their beliefs is an accurate guide to how in fact they behave, just as religious people sometimes think that secular people must lead lives of unrestrained dissipation.[70] Neither view is correct. Both sides have come to share in the American political ethos with its commitment to toleration and moderation.

A weak central government and a proliferation of diverse and independent local governments produce a country, as Tocqueville said 170 years ago, in which public action requires the mobilization of private motives. In Europe, where any public action is government action, private motives are less important. America's legacy of personal freedom has made private motives very important, and for many people religion supplies those motives.

Apart from whatever beneficial effects religion may have on health or happiness, American preoccupation with religion, especially since the emergence of the so-called Christian Right, has helped improve the level of political participation. The organization of countless religious sects that are self-governing and that must compete for members in a theological free market has expanded human involvement in democratic rule. By various lectures, essays, advertisements, and government programs we seek to encourage political participation, but what encourages it the most, especially among people who are not well off, is their religious beliefs.

The country today is more divided by religion than by income, and often that division is passionate. But the legacy of America is that, different as we are, we must live together; we must, in the words of one columnist, recognize that "there is no one vocabulary we can use to settle great issues."[71] Some religious conservatives demand that we replace teaching evolution with teaching creationism, or its latest substitute, intelligent design. Some secular liberals wanted to defy the laws of the state of California and have gay marriages. One might support a student having choices about what to study or a law authorizing gay civil unions, but the passions that are aroused by premature efforts to impose one view or the other without following the due process of the law are harmful. Even worse is the mass media's partisan coverage of such issues; rallying to support Terri Schiavo or defending heterosexual marriage will "ignite a culture war," journalists tell us, while violating state law on behalf of a secular goal is only an affirmation of human rights. There is a culture war, but unfortunately our press informs us about only one side of it.

If the left wing of the Democratic Party is to become once again a national rather than a regional organization, it must enter into a new dialogue with faith communities. This means discussing—not simply defending—abortion, and embracing a commitment to life that extends beyond opposition to the death penalty and includes people in a persistent vegetative state. It means taking seriously not only gender but also obscenity, not only racial diversity but black crime, not only gay marriage but marriage generally, not only barriers to the advancement of women but differences between women and men. If the right wing of the Republican Party wishes to remain a national party, its supporters cannot attack abortion doctors, use legislative fiat to usurp scientific knowledge, or say that judges must be held accountable for doing what an independent judiciary is supposed to do.

The effect of religion on political polarization in America is unmistakable. Religious conservatives have become an influential part of the Republican Party and secular liberals an important part of the Democratic Party. Polarization, then, reflects more than mere preferences; it embraces deeply held beliefs. That division is worrisome because it reawakens in America the tension evident in many earlier periods, such as when hostility to Catholics and Jews was politically salient. After the Second World War, we largely overcame that tension. The great strength of this country is that we have learned to live together despite our deepest passions.

Now our passions are once again dividing us. Yale Law School Professor Stephen Carter highlighted the problem when he described two black evangelical women who left the Democratic Party and embraced conservative Christian organizations because, as Carter put it, "they preferred a place that honored their faith and disdained their politics over a place that honored their politics and disdained their faith."[72] Alan Wolfe, who unlike Carter is not a religious man, sees the problem as well: "Americans love God and democracy and see no contradiction between the two. . . . Believers are full citizens of the United States, and it is time to make peace between them and the rest of America."[73]

Notes

†I am grateful for financial aid from the Earhart Foundation, the research assistance of Bryan O'Keefe and Karlyn Bowman, and comments from Peter B. Clark, John Dilulio, Roger Finke, Morton Keller, and Jon A. Shields.

1. Alan Abramowitz and Kyle Saunders, "Why Can't We All Just Get Along? The Reality of a Polarized America," *Forum* 3 (2005): 15–16.

2. The language is that of Maureen Dowd, Sidney Blumenthal, Robert Kuttner, and Thomas Friedman. A convenient summary can be found in Ramesh Ponnuru, "Secularism and Its Discontents," *National Review*, December 27, 2004, 32–35. These views are not simply those of pundits. For an uncommonly silly book that expresses these views, see Sam Harris, *The End of Faith* (New York: Norton, 2004).

3. For the left: Maureen Dowd, "DeLay, Deny, and Demagogue," *New York Times*, March 24, 2005; for the right: Randall Terry, invited by Terri Schiavo's parents to organize protests on her behalf, once said that "our goal is a Christian nation. . . . We are called by God to conquer this country . . . Theocracy means God rules." See the (Fort Wayne, IN) *News Sentinel*, August 16, 1993.

4. Wilfred McClay, "The Church of Civil Rights," *Commentary*, June 2004, 45; and David L. Chappell, *A Stone of Hope: Prophetic Religion and the Death of Jim Crow* (Chapel Hill, NC: University of North Carolina Press, 2004), chap. 6.

5. On these matters, see Stephen L. Carter, *The Culture of Disbelief* (New York: Basic Books, 1993), especially 49, 59–60, 227–28.

6. Chappell, *A Stone of Hope*, chap. 1.

7. John Dewey, cited in ibid., 13–14.

8. Lionel Trilling, *The Liberal Imagination* (New York: Doubleday Anchor Books, 1953), 9.

9. John C. Green et al., "Bringing in the Sheaves: The Christian Right and White Protestants, 1976–1996," in *Sojourners in the Wilderness*, ed. Corwin E. Smidt and James M. Penning (Lanham, MD: Rowman & Littlefield, 1997), 80.

10. Ibid., 94, 197.

11. CNN Exit Poll, 2004; Public Opinion Strategies, 2004; Pew Research Center for the People and the Press, "Religion and the Presidential Vote," December 6, 2004.

12. John C. Green et al., "The American Religious Landscape and the 2004 Presidential Vote: Increased Polarization," Pew Forum on Religious and Public Life, February 3, 2005.

13. Pippa Norris and Ronald Inglehart, *Sacred and Secular: Religion and Politics Worldwide* (Cambridge: Cambridge University Press, 2004), 72.

14. Richard Rose and Derek Unwin, "Social Cohesion, Political Parties, and Strains in Regimes," *Comparative Political Studies* 2 (1969): 7–67; Arend Lijphart, "Religious vs. Linguistic vs. Class Voting," *American Political Science Review* 73 (1979): 442–58; Russell J. Dalton, *Citizen Politics: Public Opinion and Political Parties in the United States,*

Great Britain, West Germany, and France (Chatham, NJ: Chatham House Publishers, 1988), 161–69.

15. But as Norris and Inglehart point out in *Sacred and Secular*, other studies suggest that actual church attendance in the United States is lower than these figures imply.

16. Ibid., 85.

17. See David Martin, *Tongues of Fire: The Explosion of Protestantism in Latin America* (Oxford: Blackwell, 1990), 49–55, 145, 157; Philip Jenkins, *The Next Christendom* (New York: Oxford University Press, 2002), 2–3, 56–9.

18. Berger's explanation and defense of secularization was in *The Sacred Canopy* (New York: Anchor Books, 1969), chap. 5; his recantation was in "The Desecularization of the World: A Global Overview," in *The Desecularization of the World*, ed. Peter L. Berger (Washington, DC: Ethics and Public Policy Center, 1999), chap. 1.

19. James Q. Wilson, *The Marriage Problem* (New York: HarperCollins, 2002), chap. 4; Alan Macfarlane, *The Origins of English Individualism* (New York: Cambridge University Press, 1978).

20. Steve Bruce, "The Strange Death of Protestant Britain," in *Rethinking Ethnicity*, ed. Eric P. Kaufmann (London: Routledge, 2004), 121.

21. Gregory H. Singleton, "Protestant Voluntary Organizations and the Shaping of Victorian America," in *Victorian America*, ed. Daniel Walker Howe (Philadelphia: University of Pennsylvania Press, 1976), 49–50.

22. Paul Boyer, *Urban Masses and the Moral Order in America, 1820–1920* (Cambridge, MA: Harvard University Press, 1978), 41; Thomas W. Laqueur, *Religion and Respectability: Sunday Schools and Working Class Culture, 1780–1850* (New Haven, CT: Yale University Press, 1976), 44; Callum G. Brown, *The Death of Christian Britain* (London: Routledge, 2001), 161–62.

23. There is a spirited debate among scholars as to what level of church attendance exists in this country. For an argument that attendance is less than half of what the polls suggest, see C. Kirk Hardaway, Penny Long Marler, and Mark Chaves, "What the Polls Don't Show: A Closer Look at U.S. Church Attendance," *American Sociological Review* 58 (1993): 741–52; Robert D. Woodberry, "When Surveys Lie and People Tell the Truth: How Surveys Oversample Church Attenders," *American Sociological Review* 63 (1998): 119–22; Stanley Presser and Linda Stimson, "Data Collection Mode and Social Desirability Bias in Self-Reported Religious Attendance," *American Sociological Review* 63 (1998): 137–45. Criticisms of these views are in Theodore Caplow, "The Case of the Phantom Episcopalians," *American Sociological Review* 63 (1998): 112–13; Michael Hout and Andrew Greeley, "What Church Officials' Reports Don't Show: Another Look at Church Attendance Data," *American Sociological Review* 63 (1998): 113–19; and Michael Hout and Andrew Greeley, "The Center Doesn't Hold: Church Attendance in the United States, 1940–1984," *American Sociological Review* 52 (1987): 325–45.

24. The immigrant argument is made in Steve Bruce, *God is Dead* (Oxford: Blackwell, 2002), 219–20.

25. Rodney Stark and Roger Finke, "American Religion in 1776: A Statistical Portrait," *Sociological Analysis* 49 (1988): 39–51; Rodney Finke and Roger Stark, "Turning Pews Into People: Estimating 19th Century Church Membership," *Journal for the Scientific Study of Religion* 25 (1986): 180–92.

26. By 1980, Mormons were the fifth largest denomination in the United States. See Rodney Stark, "The Rise of a New World Faith," in *Latter-day Saint Social Life*, ed. James T. Duke (Provo, UT: Brigham Young University, 1998), 16. Mormons are recruited, not in areas where religiosity is strong, but where it is weak. Cf. Rodney Stark and William S. Bainbridge, *The Future of Religion* (Berkeley, CA: University of California Press, 1985).

27. Rodney Stark, "Germans and German-American Religion: Approximating a Crucial Experiment," *Journal for the Scientific Study of Religion* 36 (1997): 182–93.

28. Jose Casanova, *Public Religions in the Modern World* (Chicago: University of Chicago Press, 1994), 29.

29. David Barrett et al., *World Christian Encyclopedia*, 2d ed. (Oxford: Oxford University Press, 2001), 284.

30. Rodney Stark and Roger Finke, *Acts of Faith: Explaining the Human Side of Religion* (Berkeley, CA: University of California Press, 2000), 228–30.

31. Martin Conway, introduction to *Political Catholicism in Europe, 1918–1965*, ed. Tom Buchanan and Martin Conway (Oxford: Clarendon Press, 1996), especially 30–31; Stathis N. Kalyvas, *The Rise of Christian Democracy in Europe* (Ithaca, NY: Cornell University Press, 1996), 258–64.

32. Alexis de Tocqueville, *Democracy in America*, ed. Phillips Bradley (New York: Alfred Knopf, 1945), 1:310, 314.

33. Andrew C. Gould, *Origins of Liberal Dominance: State, Church, and Party in Nineteenth-Century Europe* (Ann Arbor, MI: University of Michigan Press, 1999), 121–22.

34. Donald G. Swift, *Religion and the American Experience* (Armonk, NY: M. E. Sharpe, 1998), 13.

35. *Everson v. United States*, 330 U.S. 1 (1947) made the religious clauses of the First Amendment applicable to the states via the Fourteenth Amendment.

36. *Pierce v. Society of Sisters*, 268 U.S. 510 (1925). On church-state relations, see Philip Hamburger, *Separation of Church and State* (Cambridge, MA: Harvard University Press, 2002).

37. Hamburger, *Separation of Church and State*, chap. 8, 297–98.

38. The free market view of church activities is developed at length in Roger Finke and Rodney Stark, *The Churching of America, 1776–1990* (New Brunswick, NJ: Rutgers University Press, 1992) and Stark and Finke, *Acts of Faith*. I believe they are correct about the United States, but I am not convinced that their theory explains differences among countries in religious affiliations. There are too many specific political and cultural differences that must be taken into account to make any single theory useful in comparative religious politics.

39. Martin, *Tongues of Fire*, 21; E. R. Norman, *Church and Society in England, 1770–1970* (Oxford: Clarendon Press, 1976), 314–46, 364–75, 418–74.

40. David Hempton, *Methodism and Politics in British Society, 1750–1850* (London: Hutchinson, 1984), especially 58, and David Hempton, *The Religion of the People* (London: Routledge, 1996), 6–7. I am grateful to Roger Finke for these references.

41. Dean M. Kelley, *Why Conservative Churches Are Growing* (New York: Harper & Row, 1977), chap. 1. Roger Finke and Rodney Stark agree with Kelley's views but give evidence that the decline in mainline church membership began, not in the 1960s as he argued, but by the 1940s.

42. Kelley, *Why Conservative Churches Are Growing*, ix, 91–94.

43. Laurence R. Iannacone, "Why Strict Churches Are Strong," *American Journal of Sociology* 99 (1994): 1180–1211. See also Laurence R. Iannacone, Roger Finke, and Rodney Stark, "Deregulating Religion: The Economics of Church and State," *Economic Inquiry* (1997): 350–64.

44. Norris and Inglehart, *Sacred and Secular*, chap.10.

45. Laurence R. Iannacone, "The Consequences of Religious Market Structure," *Rationality and Society* 3 (1991): 156–77. Indeed, Smith made exactly this prediction in *The Wealth of Nations*, R. H. Campbell, A. S. Skinner, eds. (Oxford: Clarendon Press, 1976), 2:788–89.

46. Kelley, *Why Conservative Churches Are Growing*, 38.

47. For a summary of what the Christian Right has or has not accomplished, see Steve Bruce, *Conservative Protestant Politics* (Oxford: Oxford University Press, 1998), 164–89.

48. On the scandals afflicting Pat Robertson and various televangelists, see Steve Bruce, *Pray TV: Televangelism in America* (London: Routledge, 1990), 172–73, 198–212.

49. J. Christopher Sopher, "Divided by a Common Religion: The Christian Right in England and the United States," in *Sojourners in the Wilderness* (Lanham, MD: Rowman & Littlefield, 1997), 186.

50. Hempton, *Religion of the People*, 16.

51. Laura Berkowitz and John C. Green, "Charting the Coalition: The Local Chapters of the Ohio Christian Coalition," in *Sojourners in the Wilderness*, ed. Corwin E. Smidt and James M. Penning (Lanham, MD: Rowman & Littlefield, 1997), 42–45; Francis Fitzgerald, "A Disciplined Charging Army," *New Yorker*, May 18, 1981, 53–97.

52. Mary E. Bendyna and Clyde Wilcox, "The Christian Right Old and New," in *Sojourners in the Wilderness*, ed. Corwin E. Smidt and James M. Penning (Lanham, MD: Rowman & Littlefield, 1997), 53–55.

53. Mark J. Rozell and Clyde Wilcox, *Second Coming: The New Christian Right in Virginia Politics* (Baltimore, MD: Johns Hopkins University Press, 1996), 216–21. This view is reinforced by Jon A. Shields, *The Democratic Virtues of the Christian Right* (Princeton, NJ: Princeton University Press, 2009), a fine-grained study of conservative

Christian rhetoric and actions. According to Robert Wuthnow, "religious conservatives have accommodated to the norms of secular rationality." *The Restructuring of American Religion* (Princeton, NJ: Princeton University Press, 1988), 302.

54. Robert Wuthnow, *America and the Challenges of Religious Diversity* (Princeton, NJ: Princeton University Press, 2005), 32, 188, 198.

55. Harriet Martineau, *Society in America* (London: Saunders and Otley, 1837), 2:323.

56. John T. McGreevy, *Catholicism and American Freedom* (New York: Norton, 1993), 166-70.

57. Christian Smith, *American Evangelicalism: Embattled and Thriving* (Chicago: University of Chicago Press, 1998), 1-7.

58. "Mobilizing the Faithful," Gallup poll, December 21, 2004.

59. As quoted in Rozell and Wilcox, *Second Coming*, 10.

60. Ibid., 14.

61. Christian Smith, *Christian America? What Evangelicals Really Want* (Berkeley, CA: University of California Press, 2000), 10.

62. Smith, *American Evangelicalism*, 77. See also Wuthnow, *America and the Challenges of Religious Diversity*, 210.

63. Dale A. Matthews et al., "Religious Commitment and Health Status," *Archives of Family Medicine* 7 (1998): 118-24.

64. Byron R. Johnson et al., "Escaping From the Crime of Inner Cities: Church Attendance and Religious Salience Among Disadvantaged Youth," *Justice Quarterly* 17 (2000): 377-91. See also Richard B. Freeman, "Who Escapes?" in *The Black Youth Employment Crisis*, ed. Richard B. Freeman and H. J. Holzer (Chicago: University of Chicago Press, 1986).

65. Byron R. Johnson et al. "The 'Invisible Institution' and Black Youth Crime," *Journal of Youth and Adolescence* 29 (2000): 479-98. See also Charles R. Tittle and Michael R. Welch, "Religiosity and Deviance," *Social Forces* 61 (1983): 653-82.

66. Arland Thornton, William G. Axinn, and Daniel H. Hill, "Reciprocal Effects of Religiosity, Cohabitation, and Marriage," *American Journal of Sociology* 98 (1992): 628-51.

67. William T. Martin, "Religiosity and United States Suicide Rates, 1972-1978," *Journal of Clinical Psychology* 40 (1984): 1166-69; Steven Sack, "The Effect of Domestic Religious Individualism on Suicide, 1954-1978," *Journal of Marriage and the Family* 47 (1985): 431-47; David B. Larson and William P. Wilson, "Religious Lives of Alcoholics," *Southern Medical Journal* 73 (1980): 723-27; Robert H. Coombs, David K. Wellisch, and Fawzy I. Fawzy, "Drinking Patterns and Problems Among Female Children and Adolescents," *American Journal of Drug and Alcohol Abuse* 11 (1985): 315-48; Richard L. Gorsuch and M. C. Butler, "Initial Drug Abuse," *Psychological Bulletin*, 3 (1976): 120-37; Ron D. Hays et al., "Multistage Path Models of Adolescent Alcohol and Drug Use," *Journal of Drug Issues* 16 (1986): 357-69; M. Daum and M. A. Lavenhar, "Religiosity and Drug Use," National Institute of Drug Abuse, ADM 80939, 1980.

68. Arthur C. Brooks, "Religious Faith and Charitable Giving, *Policy Review* 121 (October/November 2003): 39–50.

69. William J. Stuntz, "Faculty Clubs and Church Pews," Tech Central Station, posted November 29, 2004, http://www.unm.edu/~pre/law/articles_advise/religious.html.

70. Alan Wolfe, *The Transformation of American Religion* (New York: Free Press, 2003), 252.

71. David Brooks, "Stuck in Lincoln's Land," *New York Times*, May 5, 2005, A27.

72. Stephen L. Carter, *The Dissent of the Governed* (Cambridge, MA.: Harvard University Press, 1998), 9.

73. Wolfe, *Transformation of American Religion*, 255.

9

Why Don't Jews Like the Christians Who Like Them?

Originally published in City Journal, Winter 2008

Religious diversity in America has produced a puzzle: the two faiths most supportive of Israel do not seem to care very much for one another.

In the United States, the two groups that most ardently support Israel are Jews and evangelical and fundamentalist Christians. Jewish support is easy to explain, but why should certain Christians, most of them politically quite conservative, be so devoted to Israel? There is a second puzzle: despite their support for a Jewish state, evangelical and fundamentalist Christians are disliked by many Jews. And a third: a large fraction of African-Americans are hostile to Israel and critical of Jews, yet Jewish voters regard blacks as their natural allies.

The evidence about evangelical attitudes is clear. In 2006, a Pew survey found that evangelical Christians were more sympathetic toward Israel than the average American was—and much more sympathetic than either mainline Protestants or secularists. In another survey, evangelical Christians proved much likelier than Catholics, Protestants, or secular types to back Israeli control of Jerusalem, endorse Israeli settlements on the West Bank, and take Israel's side in a Middle Eastern dispute. (Among every religious group, those who are most traditional are most supportive of Israel. The most orthodox Catholics and Protestants, for instance, support Israel more than their modernist colleagues do.)

Evangelical Christians have a high opinion not just of the Jewish state but of Jews as people. That Jewish voters are overwhelmingly liberal doesn't seem to bother evangelicals, despite their own conservative politics. Yet Jews don't return the favor: in one Pew survey, 42 percent of Jewish respondents expressed hostility to evangelicals and fundamentalists. As two scholars from Baruch College have shown, a much smaller fraction—about 16 percent—of the American public as a whole has similarly antagonistic feelings toward Christian fundamentalists.

The reason that conservative Christians—opposed to abortion and gay marriage and critical of political liberalism—can feel kindly toward Jewish liberals and support Israel so fervently is rooted in theology, specifically in a fundamentalist doctrine called dispensationalism. The dispensationalist outlook, which began in early nineteenth-century England, sees human history as a series of seven periods, or dispensations, in each of which God deals with man in a distinctive way. The first, before Adam's fall, was the era of innocence; the second, from Adam to Noah, the era of conscience; the third, from Noah to Abraham, of government; the fourth, from Abraham to Moses, of patriarchy; the fifth, from Moses to Jesus, of Mosaic law; and the sixth, from Jesus until today, of grace. The seventh and final dispensation, yet to come, will be the Millennium, an earthly paradise.

For dispensationalists, the Jews are God's chosen people. For the Millennium to come, they must be living in Israel; the Temple in Jerusalem will rise again at the time of Armageddon. On the eve of that final battle, the Antichrist will appear—probably in the form of a seeming peacemaker. Fundamentalists differ over who the Antichrist will be (at one time he was thought to be Nero, at another time the pope, and today a few have suggested the secretary general of the United Nations), but dispensationalists agree that he will deceive the people, occupy the Temple, rule in the name of God, and ultimately be defeated by the Messiah. Many dispensationalists believe that how a person treats Israel will profoundly influence his eternal destiny.

Christian dispensationalists were early Zionists and continue to support Israel today, for it is there, they believe, that Christ will return. William Blackstone, a well-known dispensationalist and the author of *Jesus Is Coming*, called in 1891 for a Jewish state in Palestine, five years before Theodor Herzl and six years before the first Zionist Congress. Blackstone got more than four hundred dignitaries to sign his document, including the chief justice of the Supreme Court, the speaker of the House, John D. Rockefeller, J. P. Morgan, and several other prominent Americans, almost all of them Christians. After

President Benjamin Harrison ignored the petition, Blackstone tried again in 1916 with President Woodrow Wilson, who was more sympathetic—and who supported the British foreign minister, Arthur Balfour, a devout Protestant, when in 1917 he issued his famous declaration calling for a Jewish home in Palestine.

Evangelical and fundamentalist Christian preachers enthusiastically promote this pro-Israel vision. In a study of preachers in nineteen denominations, political scientist James Guth of Furman University found that evangelicals were much likelier to back Israel in their sermons than mainline Protestants or Catholics were, a difference that persisted after controlling for age, sex, party identification, and type of media used to reach congregations. Guth also showed that self-described evangelicals who attended church regularly, and thus heard their ministers' sermons, were much more inclined to support Israel than were believers who did not attend regularly.

Evangelical preachers are reinforced by popular Christian books. In 1970, Hal Lindsey published *The Late Great Planet Earth*; in 1995, Tim LaHaye and Jerry Jenkins followed with *Left Behind: A Novel of the Earth's Last Days*, and went on to write eleven more volumes on the same theme. Lindsey can claim more than thirty-five million sales, and the *Left Behind* books have sold sixty million. These best sellers tell the dispensationalist story, discuss Armageddon, and argue for the protection of Jews and of Israel. According to Lindsey, the book of Revelations and related biblical sources predict that there will be "a seven-year period climaxed by the visible return of Jesus Christ"—but that this period will not commence until the Jewish people have reestablished their nation in their ancient homeland.

Whatever one makes of his prediction, Lindsey is unambiguous about the importance of Israel to him—and, by extension, to his millions of readers. Reinforcing the preachers and writers are various pro-Israel evangelical organizations, including Bridges for Peace, the International Christian Embassy Jerusalem, and the National Christian Leadership Conference for Israel.

Mainstream Protestant groups, such as the National Council of Churches and the Middle East Council of Churches, have a very different attitude toward Israel. The NCC, for example, refused to support Israel during the Six-Day War in 1967, and immediately afterward began to protest victorious Israel's expansion of its territory. From that point on, the NCC's positions ran closely with Arab opinion, urging American contact with the Palestine Liberation Organization, for instance, and denouncing the Camp David Accords because they supposedly ignored the Palestinians' national ambitions. In 2004, the Presbyterian Church decided to study a proposal to divert its investments from firms doing business with Israel. Within a year, the Episcopal Church, the United Church of Christ, and parts of the Methodist Church followed suit. Paul Charles Merkley sums up the situation in his book about Christian Zionism: mainline Protestant churches' "respectable leadership had backed away from Israel; all of her constant friends were seated below the salt."

Why do mainline Protestant leaders oppose Israel? That question becomes harder to answer when one recalls that Israel is a democratic nation with vigorously independent courts that has not only survived brutal attacks by its Arab neighbors but provided a prosperous home for the children of many Holocaust survivors. As with any other nation, Israel has pursued policies that one can challenge. Some may criticize its management of the West Bank, for example, or its attacks on Hamas leaders. But these concerns are trivial compared with Iran's announced desire to wipe Israel off the map by using every weapon at its disposal, including (eventually) a nuclear one.

The answer, I think, is that many Christian liberals see Israel as blocking the aspirations of the oppressed—who, they have decided, include the Palestinians. Never mind that the Palestinians support suicide bombers and rocket attacks against Israel; never mind that the Palestinians cannot form a competent government; never mind that they wish to occupy Israel "from the sea to the river." It is enough that they seem oppressed, even though much of the oppression is self-inflicted.

After the Marxist claims about the proletariat proved false and capitalism was vindicated as the best way to achieve economic affluence, leftists had to stop pretending that they could accomplish much with state-owned factories and national economic plans. As a result, the oppressed replaced the proletariat as the Left's object of affection. The enemy became, not capitalists, but successful nations.

That shift in focus has received encouragement from certain American academics, such as Noam Chomsky, and from the European press, including the BBC, the *Guardian*, the *Evening Standard*, and *Le Monde*. All tend to denounce Israel in the most unrestrained terms. When Israeli ground forces seeking to root out terrorists hiding in a Jenin refugee camp lost twenty-three soldiers and killed fifty-two Palestinians, the British writer A. N. Wilson, uninterested in the facts, called the episode a "massacre" and a "genocide." There will always be those whom the Left considers enemies; Israel has merely replaced John D. Rockefeller at the top of the list.

But why do so many Jewish groups and voters abhor their Christian evangelical allies? To answer that question carefully, we would need data that distinguish among Orthodox, Conservative, Reform, and secular Jews. It is quite possible that Orthodox Jews welcome evangelical support while Reform and secular ones oppose it, but I could find no data on which to base a firm conclusion. Most Jews are political liberals, devoted to the Democratic Party and liberal causes generally. As Milton Himmelfarb once put it, "Jews earn like Episcopalians and vote like Puerto Ricans." Such voting habits are not hard to explain in a population that historically includes victims of discrimination, oppression, and mass murder. By contrast, evangelicals tend to be conservatives to whom politics seems less important than their dispensationalist beliefs.

That for many American Jews liberal politics trumps other considerations—including worries about anti-Semitism—becomes clearer in light of other data. The most anti-Semitic group in America is African-Americans. This wasn't always the case. Many early black leaders, including W. E. B. Du Bois and Ralph Bunche, were quite supportive of American Jews. Du Bois even criticized Bunche for being "insufficiently pro-Zionist." The NAACP endorsed the creation of Israel in 1948, and the Jewish state received continued support from Paul Robeson, Bayard Rustin, and Martin Luther King, Jr. But by the time of the 1967 war, much of that leadership had left the scene. Stokely Carmichael, H. Rap Brown, James Forman, Malcolm X, and Shirley Du Bois (widow of W. E. B. Du Bois) were critical of Israel. At a New Left convention in the late 1960s, black delegates insisted on passing a resolution condemning the "imperialist Zionist war." Nowadays, according to several polls, about one-third of U.S. blacks have very anti-Semitic attitudes, and this hasn't changed since at least 1964, when the first such poll was conducted. And it has been African-American leaders, not white evangelicals, who have made anti-Semitic remarks most conspicuously. Everyone recalls Jesse Jackson's reference to New York as "Hymietown"; and Louis Farrakhan, a great admirer of Hitler, has called Jews "bloodsuckers."

Yet African-American voters are liberals, and so often get a pass from their Jewish allies. To Jews, blacks are friends and evangelicals enemies, whatever their respective dispositions toward Jews and Israel.

But another reason, deeper than Jewish and evangelical differences over abortion, school prayer, and gay marriage, may underlie Jewish dislike of Christian fundamentalists. Though evangelical Protestants are supportive of Israel and tolerant of Jews, in the eyes of their liberal critics they are hostile to the essential elements of a democratic regime. They believe that the United States was founded as a Christian nation and worry about the decay of morality; they must wish, therefore, to impose a conservative moral code, alter the direction of the country so that it conforms to God's will, require public schools to teach Christian beliefs, and crush the rights of minorities.

Christian Smith, a sociology professor at the University of North Carolina, analyzed four surveys of self-identified evangelicals and found that, while they do think that America was founded as a Christian nation and fear that the country has lost its moral bearings, these views are almost exactly the same as those held by nonevangelical Americans. Evangelicals, like other Americans, oppose having public schools teach Christian values, oppose having public school teachers lead students in vocal prayers, and oppose a constitutional amendment declaring the country a Christian nation. Evangelicals deny that there is one correct Christian view on most political issues, deny that Jews must answer for allegedly killing Christ, deny that laws protecting free speech go too far, and reject the idea that whites should be able to keep blacks out of their neighborhoods. They overwhelmingly agree that Jews and Christians share the same values and can live together in harmony. Evangelicals strongly oppose abortion and gay marriage, but in almost every other respect are like other Americans.

Whatever the reason for Jewish distrust of evangelicals, it may be a high price to pay when Israel's future, its very existence, is in question. Half of all Protestants in the country describe themselves as evangelical, or born-again, Christians, making up about one-quarter of *all* Americans (though they constitute only 16 percent of white Christian voters in the Northeast). Jews, by contrast, make up less than 2 percent of the U.S. population, and that percentage will shrink: as many as half of all Jews marry non-Jews. When it comes to helping secure Israel's survival, the tiny Jewish minority in America should not reject the help offered by a group that is ten times larger and whose views on the central propositions of a democratic society are much like everybody else's. No good can come from repeating the 1926 assertion of H. L. Mencken that fundamentalist Christians are "yokels" and "morons."

10

What Makes a Terrorist?

Originally published in City Journal, Winter 2004

Terrorists, we often suppose, are a few radical jihadists trained abroad; of late we have learned that many are homegrown murderers who may acquire their techniques abroad but who came to hate America while living here. There are no easy explanations for why someone becomes a terrorist: it is usually not economic disadvantage or personal tragedy that is responsible but instead a psychological quirk reinforced by indoctrination from an imam, the influence of like-minded friends, and the teachings of jihadist Web pages.

Until the nineteenth century, religion was usually the only acceptable justification for terror. It is not hard to understand why: religion gives its true believers an account of the good life and a way of recognizing evil. If you believe that evil in the form of wrong beliefs and mistaken customs weakens or corrupts a life ordained by God, you are under a profound obligation to combat that evil. If you enjoy the companionship of like-minded believers, combating that evil can require that you commit violent, even suicidal, acts.

The Thuggee cult of India during its several centuries of existence may have slowly strangled a million people as sacrifices to the Hindu goddess Kali. The Thugs had no political objective and, when caught, looked forward to their execution as a quick route to paradise.

In the Muslim world, one kind of terrorism, assassination, has existed since shortly after the death of the prophet Muhammad. Of his early successors, three were killed with daggers. The very word "assassin" comes from a group founded by Hasan Ibn al-Sabbah, whose devotees, starting in the eleventh century, spread terror throughout the Muslim world until they were virtually exterminated two centuries later. They killed rival Sunni Muslims, probably in large numbers. Perhaps one-third of all Muslim caliphs have been killed.

The Assassins were perhaps the world's first terrorists in two senses. They did not seek simply to change rulers through murder but to institute an entirely new social system by changing an allegedly corrupt Sunni regime into a supposedly ideal Shiite one. Moreover, the Assassins carried out proto–suicide attacks; using only daggers, they were very likely to be captured and executed, often after gruesome torture. Murder was an act of piety, and as Bernard Lewis has suggested, surviving such a mission was often viewed as shameful.

In modern times, we also see killers with religious motives, a desire to overthrow a corrupt regime, and a willingness to die in carrying out their attack. These have taken the lives of the presidents of Syria and of Sri Lanka; two prime ministers each of Iran and India; the presidents of Aden, Afghanistan, and South Yemen; the president-elect of Lebanon and the president of Egypt; and countless judges and political leaders. But religiously oriented violence has by no means been confined to Islam. In the United States, abortion clinics have been bombed and their doctors shot because, the perpetrators believed, the Christian Bible commands it. Jim Jones killed or required the suicide of his own followers at his camp in Guyana, and David Koresh did nothing to prevent the mass death of his followers at Waco. As Blaise Pascal put it, "men never do evil so openly and contentedly as when they do it from religious conviction."

Bruce Hoffman, a terrorism expert at the RAND Corporation, has found that religiously motivated suicide attacks kill four times as many people per incident as do other forms of terrorism; since September 2000, they have taken about 750 lives—not including the 3,000 who died from the 9/11 suicide attacks. Of course, most religious people have nothing to do with terror; some terrorist attacks, including suicide attacks, have no religious impulse (the Japanese kamikaze attacks and the attacks of the Tamil Tigers in Sri Lanka); and some Middle Eastern terrorist groups are secular (Fatah). That said, religious belief, and especially a certain interpretation of the Muslim religion, has come to dominate the motives of suicide terrorists, even when religious aspirations do not govern the organizations that recruit them.

Crazy, Poor, or Desperate?

Acts of terrorism, however motivated, baffle people who cannot imagine doing these things themselves. This bafflement often leads us to assume that terrorists are either mentally deranged or products of a hostile environment.

In a powerful essay, Cynthia Ozick describes "the barbarous Palestinian societal invention": recruiting children to blow themselves up. She argues that this is an act of "anti-instinct," because it is contrary to the drive to live. She is correct to say that this recruitment is not psychopathological, but not quite right to say that it defies instinct. It defies some instincts but is in accord with others.

To explain why people join these different terrorist groups, let me make some distinctions. One, suggested by Professor Jerrold Post at George Washington University, is between anarchic ideologues and nationalists. Anarchist or ideological groups include the Red Army Faction in Germany (popularly known as the Baader-Meinhof gang), the Red Brigades in Italy, and the Weathermen in America. The German government carried out a massive inquiry into the Red Army Faction and some right-wing terrorist groups in the early 1980s. (Since it was done in Germany, you will not be surprised to learn that the published report ran to four volumes.) The Red Army members were middle-class people, who came, in about 25 percent of the cases, from broken families. Over three-fourths said they had severe conflicts with their parents. About one-third had been convicted in juvenile court. They wanted to denounce "the establishment" and bourgeois society generally, and joined peer groups that led them steadily into more radical actions that in time took over their lives. Italians in the Red Brigades had comparable backgrounds.

Ideological terrorists offer up no clear view of the world they are trying to create. They speak vaguely about bringing people into some new relationship with one another but never tell us what that relationship might be. Their goal is destruction, not creation. To the extent they are Marxists, this vagueness is hardly surprising, since Marx himself never described the world he hoped to create, except with a few glittering but empty generalities.

Before I turn to the nationalists, let me make a further distinction: in Germany, left-wing terrorists, such as the Red Army Faction, were much better educated, had a larger fraction of women as members, and were better organized than were right-wing terrorists. Similar differences have existed in the United States between, say, the Weather Underground and the Aryan Nation. Left-wing terrorists often have a well-rehearsed ideology (even if no clear plan for how to organize the world after their violence); right-wing ones are more likely to be pathological.

I am not entirely certain why this difference should exist. One possibility is that right-wing terrorist organizations are looking backward at a world they think has been lost, whereas left-wing ones are looking ahead at a world they hope will arrive. Higher education is useful to those who wish to imagine a future but of little value to those who think they know the past. Leftists get from books and professors a glimpse of the future, and they struggle to create it. Right-wingers base their discontent on a sense of the past, and they work to restore it. To join the Ku Klux Klan or the Aryan Nation, it is only necessary that members suppose that it is good to oppress blacks or Catholics or Jews; to join the Weather Underground, somebody had to teach recruits that a decadent and oppressive bourgeois society can be replaced by something joyous and better.

Nationalistic and religious terrorists are a very different matter. The fragmentary research that has been done on them makes clear that they are rarely in conflict with their parents; on the contrary, they seek to carry out in extreme ways ideas learned at home. Moreover, they usually have a very good idea of the kind of world they wish to create: it is the world given to them by their religious or nationalistic leaders. These leaders, of course, may completely misrepresent the doctrines they espouse, but the misrepresentation acquires a commanding power.

Marc Sageman at the University of Pennsylvania has analyzed what we know so far about members of al-Qaida. Unlike ideological terrorists, they felt close to their families and described them as intact and caring. They rarely had criminal records; indeed, most were devout Muslims. The great majority were married; many had children. None had any obvious signs of mental disorder. The appeal of al-Qaida was that the group provided a social community that helped them define and resist the decadent values of the West. The appeal of that community seems to have been especially strong to the men who had been sent abroad to study and found themselves alone and underemployed.

A preeminent nationalistic terrorist, Sabri al-Bana (otherwise known as Abu Nidal), was born to a wealthy father in Jaffa, and through his organization, the Fatah Revolutionary Council, also known as the Abu Nidal Organization, sought to destroy Israel and to attack Palestinian leaders who showed any inclination to engage in diplomacy. He was hardly a member of the wretched poor.

Alan B. Krueger and Jitka Maleckova have come to similar conclusions about nationalistic or religious terrorists from their analysis of deceased soldiers in Hezbollah, the Iran-sponsored Shiite fighting group in Lebanon. Compared with the Lebanese population generally, the Hezbollah soldiers were relatively well-to-do and well educated. In those respects they were much like Israeli Jews who were members of the Gush Emunim ("bloc of the faithful") group that tried to blow up the Dome of the Rock mosque in Jerusalem: well paid, well educated, and of course deeply religious.

Singaporean psychologists who studied thirty-one members of the terrorist organization Jemaah Islamiyah found them normal in most respects. All were male, had average to above-average intelligence, and held jobs ranging from taxi driver to engineer. As with al-Qaida and Hezbollah members, they did not come from unstable families, nor did they display any peculiar desire toward suicidal behavior. Though graduates of secular schools, they attached great importance to religion.

Of late, women have been recruited for terrorist acts—a remarkable development in the Islamic world, where custom keeps women in subordinate roles. Female suicide bombers can easily hide their identities and disguise themselves as Israelis by wearing tight, Western clothing. Security sources in Israel have suggested that some of these women became suicide bombers to expunge some personal dishonor; death in a holy cause could wash away the shame of divorce, infertility, or promiscuity. According to some accounts, a few women have deliberately been seduced and then emotionally blackmailed into becoming bombers.

That terrorists themselves are reasonably well-off does not by itself disprove the argument that terrorism springs from poverty and ignorance. Terrorists might simply be a self-selected elite, who hope to serve the needs of an impoverished and despondent populace—in which case, providing money and education to the masses would be the best way to prevent terrorism.

From what we know now, however, this theory appears to be false. Krueger and Maleckova compared terrorist incidents in the Middle East with changes in the gross domestic product of the region and found that the number of such incidents per year increased as economic conditions improved. On the eve of the intifada that began in 2000, the unemployment rate among Palestinians in the West Bank and Gaza Strip was falling, and the Palestinians thought that economic conditions were improving. The same economic conditions existed at the time of the 1988 intifada. Terror did not spread as the economy got worse but as it got better.

This study complements the findings of Franklin L. Ford, whose book *Political Murder* covers terrorist acts from ancient times down to the 1980s. Assassinations, he finds, were least common in fifth-century Athens, during the Roman republic, and in eighteenth-century Europe—periods in which "a certain quality of balance, as between authority and forbearance" was reinforced by a commitment to "customary rights." Terrorism has not corresponded to high levels of repression or social injustice or high rates of ordinary crime. It seems to occur, Ford suggests, in periods of partial reform, popular excitement, high expectations, and impatient demands for still more rapid change.

If terrorists—suicide bombers and other murderers of innocent people—are not desperate, perhaps they are psychologically disturbed. But I cannot think of a single major scholar studying this matter who has found any psychosis. Terrorists are likely to be different from nonterrorists, but not because of any obvious disease.

In short, recruiting religiously inspired or nationalistically oriented terrorists does not seem to rely on finding individuals who suffer from psychosis, material deprivation, or family rejection. It may not even rely much on well-known, high-status leaders. Among West Bank and Gaza Palestinians, for example, there is broad support for suicide bombings and a widespread belief that violence has helped the Palestinian cause, even though as late as June 2003 only about one-third of all Palestinians thought Yasser Arafat was doing a good job. Indeed, his popularity has declined since the intifada began.

Methods of Recruitment

The key to terrorist recruitment, obviously, is the group that does the recruitment. Jerrold Post conducted lengthy interviews with an Abu Nidal terrorist named Omar Rezaq, who had skyjacked an Egyptair plane and killed five passengers, two of them women, before an Egyptian rescue team captured him. The interviews sought to test the defense counsel's claim that Rezaq suffered from post-traumatic stress disorder and so did not appreciate the wrongfulness of his actions. Post found no such disease.

He met instead a thoroughly calm, professional man, who had a happy childhood devoid of poverty, and who moved with his mother to a refugee camp following the 1967 Arab-Israeli War. At school he encountered a radical Palestinian teacher (a PLO member) who imbued him with a hatred of Israel and helped him join a camp where, at age twelve, he began receiving military training. From there he went to a technical school sponsored by the United Nations. After being drafted into the Jordanian army, Rezaq deserted and joined Fatah, where he learned about Zionism and got more military training. He was sent on military missions against Israel, but periods of inactivity made him discontented.

In time, searching for a stronger commitment, he joined Abu Nidal, which ordered him to seize an airliner and hold it until Egypt released certain activists from prison. After the plane he had seized landed in Malta, Rezaq began executing passengers, beginning with two Israelis (they were the enemy) and three Americans (they supported the enemy). Before he could kill more, a rescue team stormed the plane and captured him.

Rezaq spoke to Professor Post in a calm, orderly, unemotional way. He thought of himself as a soldier and of the people he shot as enemies. He realized that his actions were crimes—that was why he wore a ski mask—but he did not think they were wrong: he was, after all, fighting Zionism. The notion that he was mentally ill was absurd: Abu Nidal, a highly professional group, would have long since weeded him out. Abu Nidal had killed or injured many people in massacres at the Rome and Vienna airports and gravely wounded the Israeli ambassador to Great Britain: you do not accomplish these things by relying on psychotics.

While some suicide bombers have been the victims of blackmail, and some have been led to believe, wrongly, that the bombs in their trucks would go off after they had left them, my sense is that most recruitment today relies on small-group pressure and authoritative leaders. Anyone who took social science courses in college will surely remember the famous experiments by Stanley Milgram. In the 1960s, Milgram, then a professor at

Yale, recruited ordinary people to help in a project purporting to improve human memory. The apparent subject, who was to be punished when he seemed unable to remember words read aloud to him, was really a confederate of Milgram's. The true subjects were those answering the ad, who thought they were administering the punishment—"shocks" ranging from 15 to 450 volts, with the high end of the scale clearly marked "Danger—Severe Shock."

About two-thirds of the subjects Milgram recruited went all the way to 450 volts, even as the supposed subject screamed in pretended pain. Only two things made a difference in the choice of the other third: the absence of a clear authority figure and the presence of rebellious peers. Without these modifications, almost everybody decided to "follow orders." This study suggests to me that, rightly managed, a cohesive group with an authoritative leader can find people who will do almost anything.

Terrorist cells, whether or not they have heard of Stanley Milgram's project, understand these rules. They expose members to unchallenged authority figures and quickly weed out anyone who might be rebellious. They get rid of doubts by getting rid of the doubters. This is not very different from how the military maintains morale under desperate conditions. Soldiers fight because their buddies fight. Heroism usually derives not from some deep heroic "urge" or from thoughts of Mom, apple pie, and national ideology, but from the example of others who are fighting.

Milgram did not train terrorists; he showed that the instinct Cynthia Ozick neglected—the instinct to be part of a team—can be as powerful as, or even overpower, the one that tells us to be decent to other people. But suppose Milgram had been the leader of a terrorist sect and had recruited obedient followers; suppose teachings in the schools and mass propaganda supported his group. There is almost no limit to what he could have accomplished using his recruits. They might not have been clinically ill, but they would have been incorporated into a psychopathological movement.

The central fact about terrorists is not that they are deranged, but that they are not alone. Palestinians are recruited by Hamas, the Palestinian Islamic Jihad, and the al-Aqsa Martyrs Brigade, among others. In Singapore, recruitment begins with attendance at religious schools. The ardent and compliant are drawn into Jemaah Islamiyah, where they associate with others like themselves. Being in the group gives each member a sense of special esteem and exclusivity, reinforced by the use of secrecy, code names, and specialized training. Then group members are offered the chance to be martyrs if they die in a jihad. Everywhere, leaders strengthen the bombers' commitment by isolating them in safe houses and by asking them to draft last testaments and make videotapes for their families in which they say farewell.

An End to Terrorism?

Given terrorism's long history, one must wonder whether it accomplishes its goals. For some ideological terrorists, of course, there are scarcely any clear goals that can be accomplished. But for many assassins and religious terrorists, there are important goals, such as ending tyranny, spreading a religious doctrine, or defeating a national enemy.

By these standards, terrorism does not work. Franklin Ford concluded his long history of political murders by saying that, with one or two possible exceptions, assassinations have not produced results consonant with the aims of the assassin. Walter Laqueur, in his shorter review of the matter, comes to the same conclusion: of the fifty prime ministers and heads of state killed between 1945 and 1985, it is hard to think of one whose death changed a state's policies.

Bernard Lewis argues that even the original Assassins failed: they never succeeded in overthrowing the social order or replacing Sunnis with Shiites. In a study of suicide terrorism from 1983 through 2001, Robert A. Pape found that while it "has achieved modest or very limited goals, it has so far failed to compel target democracies to abandon goals central to national wealth or security."

One reason it does not work can be found in studies of Israeli public opinion. During 1979, there were 271 terrorist incidents in Israel and the territories it administers, resulting in the deaths of 23 people and the injuring of 344 more. Public opinion surveys clearly showed that these attacks deeply worried Israelis, but their fear, instead of leading them to endorse efforts at reconciliation, produced a toughening of attitudes and a desire to see the perpetrators dealt with harshly. The intifada has produced exactly the same result in Israel.

But if terrorism does not change the views of the victims and their friends, then it is possible that campaigns against terrorism will not change the views of terrorists and the people who support them. Many social scientists have come to just this conclusion.

In the 1970s, I attended meetings at a learned academy where people wondered what could be done to stop the terrorism of the German Red Army Faction and the Italian Red Brigades. The general conclusion was that no counterattacks would work. To cope with terrorism, my colleagues felt, one must deal with its root causes.

I was not convinced. My doubts stemmed, I suppose, from my own sense that dealing with the alleged root causes of crime would not work as well as simply arresting criminals. After all, we do not know much about root causes, and most of the root causes we can identify cannot be changed in a free society—or possibly in any society.

The German and Italian authorities, faced with a grave political problem, decided not to change root causes but to arrest the terrorists. That strategy, accompanied by the collapse of East Germany and its support for terrorists, worked. Within a few years the Red Army Faction and the Red Brigades were extinct. In the United States, the Weather Underground died after its leaders were arrested.

But Islamic terrorism poses a much more difficult challenge. These terrorists live and work among people sympathetic to their cause. Those arrested will be replaced; those killed will be honored. Opinion polls in many Islamic nations show great support for anti-Israeli and anti-American terrorists. Terrorists are like the guerrillas described by Mao Zedong, who live among the peaceful populace as fish live in the sea. To cope with terrorism, we may have to cope with that sea.

The relentless vilification of Jews, Israel, and Zionism by much of the Muslim press and in many Muslim schools has produced a level of support for terrorism that vastly exceeds the backing that American or European terrorists ever enjoyed. Over 75 percent of all Palestinians supported a recent intifada and endorsed the 2003 bombing of Maxim, a restaurant in Haifa. With suicide bombers regarded as martyrs, the number of new recruits has apparently increased. The sea of support for anti-Israel terror is much vaster and deeper than what surrounded the Baader-Meinhof gang.

Imagine what it would have been like to eliminate the Baader-Meinhof gang if most West Germans believed that democracy was evil and that Marxism was the wave of the future; if the Soviet Union paid a large sum to the family of every killed or captured gang member; if West German students attended schools that taught the evils of democracy and regarded terrorists as heroes; if several West German states were governed by the equivalent of al Fatah or Hamas; and if there were a German version of Gaza, housing thousands of angry Germans who believed they had a right of return to some homeland.

On the other hand, support for resistance is not the same as support for an endless war. An opinion survey done in November 2002 by the Palestinian Center for Policy and Survey Research showed that over three-fourths of the Palestinians in Gaza and the West Bank supported a mutual cessation of violence between Israel and Palestinians and backed reconciliation between Israelis and a newly created Palestinian state. A majority favored the Palestinian Authority taking measures to prevent armed attacks against Israeli civilians. Another poll found that about half of all Palestinians wanted both the intifada and negotiations with Israel to go forward simultaneously, while 15 percent favored negotiations alone.

These facts, rarely mentioned in the American press, suggest how empty are the statements of many Middle Eastern and European leaders, who incessantly tell us that ending terrorism requires "solving" the Palestinian question by dealing with Palestinian leaders. These claims, often made to satisfy internal political needs, fail to recognize how disliked Arafat is by his own people, and how eager these people are for a government that respects the governed and avoids corruption.

But more complex than dealing with popular support for terrorism is dealing with a state that sponsors or accommodates terrorism. In that case, it is necessary to make clear that the state's leaders will suffer serious pain as a consequence of that accommodation. Though many people take exception to it, I think President Bush was right to condemn certain nations as being part of an "axis of evil," and to put leaders on notice that they cannot fund or encourage Hamas, al-Qaida, or Hezbollah without paying a heavy price for it. Iraq has learned how high that price can be.

The Israeli government is trying to impose a high price on the Palestinian Authority because of its tolerance of and support for terrorist acts in Israel. It is too early to tell whether this effort will succeed. Arrests or deterrence, after all, cannot readily prevent suicide bombings, though good intelligence can reduce them, and seizing leaders can perhaps hamper them. The presence of the Israeli Defense Forces in Palestinian areas and the construction of the physical barrier between Palestine and Israel almost surely explain the recent reduction in suicide attacks, but no such presence, costly as it is, can reduce the number to zero. As Palestinian hostility toward Israel grows, reinforced by what is taught in Palestinian schools, recruiting suicide bombers becomes much easier.

The larger question, of course, is whether ending terrorism requires a new political arrangement. In the case of the Israeli-Palestinian issue, the Palestinian people must grant Israel the right to a secure existence in exchange for being given their own country. There may be popular support among both Israelis and Palestinians for such an arrangement, but it is not obvious that political leaders of either side can endorse such a strategy. As the level of terrorism and state action grows, the opportunities for dialogue diminish, and public confidence that any new dialogue will produce meaningful results declines. No one has yet found a way to manage this difficulty.

11

The Reform Islam Needs

Originally published in City Journal, *Autumn 2002*

Why did Islamic countries that once led the world in art and philosophy lose ground to the West? The answer, in part, is that the Islamic faith prevented the growth of science, technology, and free markets, while the West—having a religion that inspired the soul but did not constrain the mind—embraced it.

We are engaged in a struggle to defeat terrorism. I have no advice on how to win that struggle, but I have some thoughts as to why it exists. The struggle exists, I think, because the West has mastered the problem of reconciling religion and freedom, while several Middle Eastern nations have not. The story of that mastery and that failure occupies several centuries of human history, in which one dominant culture, the world of Islam, was displaced by a new culture, that of the West.

Reconciling religion and freedom has been the most difficult political task most nations have faced. It is not hard to see why. People who believe that there is one set of moral rules superior to all others, laid down by God and sometimes enforced by the fear of eternal punishment, will understandably expect their nation to observe and impose these rules; to do otherwise would be to repudiate deeply held convictions, offend a divine being, and corrupt society. This is the view of many Muslims; it was also the view of Pope Leo XIII, who said in 1888 that men find freedom in obedience to the authority of God, and of the provost of Oriel College, Oxford, who informed a faculty member in 1848 that "you were not born for speculation" but to "serve God and serve man." If you think that there is one God who expects people to confess beliefs, say prayers, observe fasts, and receive sacraments, it would be impious, indeed scandalously wrong, to permit the state to ignore beliefs, prayers, fasts, and sacraments.

In furtherance of these views, Queen Mary executed three hundred Protestants, England and France expelled Jews, Ferdinand and Isabella expelled from Spain both Moors and Jews, the Spanish Inquisition tortured and executed a few thousand alleged heretics, and books were destroyed and scholars threatened for advancing theologically incorrect theories.

During this time, Islam was a vast empire stretching from western Africa into India—an empire that valued learning, prized scholars, maintained great libraries, and preserved the works of many ancient writers. But within three centuries, this greatest civilization on the face of the earth was in retreat, and the West was rising to produce a civilization renowned for its commitment to personal liberty, scientific expertise, political democracy, and free markets.

Freedom of conscience made the difference. In an old world where knowledge came from libraries, and scientific experiments were rare, freedom would not be so important. But in the new world, knowledge and all that it could produce came from the sharp challenge of competing ideas tested by standards of objective evidence. In Istanbul, Muslims printed no book until 1729, and thereafter only occasionally. By contrast, the West began publishing books three centuries earlier, and emphasized that the path to knowledge was through doubt and self-criticism. Of course, doubt and self-criticism can become, as William Bennett has observed, a self-destructive fetish, but short of that calamity, they are the source of human progress.

The central question is not why freedom of conscience failed to come to much of the Islamic world, but why it came at all to the West. Though Westerners will conventionally assign great weight to the arguments made by the defenders of freedom, I do not think that the ideas of Milton, Locke, Erasmus, and Spinoza—though important—were decisive.

What made religious toleration and later freedom of conscience possible in England was not theoretical argument but political necessity. It was necessary, first in England and later in America and much of Europe, because rulers trying to govern nations could not do so without granting freedom to people of different faiths. In the words of Herbert Butterfield, toleration was "the last policy that remained when it had proved impossible to go on fighting any longer."

The fighting occurred because different religions struggled to control nations. Here lay the chief difference between Islam and the West: Islam was a land of one religion and few states, while the West was a land of many states that were acquiring many religions. In the sixteenth century, people in England thought of themselves chiefly as Englishmen before they thought of themselves as Protestants, and those in France saw themselves as Frenchmen before they saw themselves as Catholics. In most of Islam—in Arabia and northern Africa, certainly—people saw themselves as Muslims before they thought of themselves as members of any state; indeed, states hardly existed in this world until European colonial powers created them by drawing somewhat arbitrary lines on a map.

The Muslim faith was divided into the Sunni and the Shiite; but Christianity was soon divided into four branches. The Protestant Reformation created not only Lutheranism but its archrival, Calvinism, which now joined the Roman Catholic and Greek Orthodox Churches as Christian sects.

Lutherans, like Catholics, were governed by a priesthood, but Calvinists were ruled by congregations, and so they proclaimed not only a sterner faith but a distinctive political philosophy. The followers of Luther and Calvin had little interest in religious liberty; they wanted to replace a church they detested with one that they admired. But in doing so, they helped bring about religious wars. Lutheran mobs attacked Calvinist groups in the streets of Berlin, and thousands of Calvinists were murdered in the streets of Paris. In 1555, the Peace of Augsburg settled the religious wars briefly with the phrase *cuius regio, eius religio*—meaning that people in each state or principality would have the religion of their ruler. If you didn't like your prince's religion, you had to move somewhere else.

But the problem grew worse as more dissident groups appeared. To the quarrels between Catholics, Calvinists, and Lutherans were added challenges from Anabaptists, Quakers, and Unitarians. These sects had their own passionate defenders, and they helped start many struggles. And so wars broke out again, all advancing religious claims overlaid with imperial, dynastic, and material objectives.

In France, Catholics killed twenty thousand Huguenots, three thousand in Paris alone. When the Peace of Westphalia settled the wars of the sixteenth century in 1648, it reaffirmed the old doctrine of following the religion of your ruler, but added an odd new doctrine that permitted some liberty of conscience. As C. V. Wedgwood put it, men had begun to grasp "the essential futility of putting the beliefs of the mind to the judgment of the sword."

In England, people were both exhausted by war and worried about following a ruler's orders on matters of faith. Oliver Cromwell, the leader of the successful Presbyterian revolt against the king, was a stern believer in his own faith, but he recognized that his beliefs alone would not enable him to govern; he had to have allies of other faiths. He persuaded Parliament to allow liberty "to all who fear God," provided they did not disturb the peace, and he took steps to readmit Jews into the country and to moderate attacks on the Quakers.

When Cromwell's era ended and Charles II took the throne, he brought back with him his Anglican faith, and challenged this arrangement. After he died, James II came to the throne and tried to reestablish Roman Catholicism. When William of Orange invaded the country from Holland in 1688, James II fled, and in time William and his wife, Mary, became rulers. Mary, a Protestant, was the daughter of James II, a Catholic. A lot of English people must have wondered how they were supposed to cope with religious choice if a father and daughter in the royal family could not get the matter straight.

In 1689, Parliament passed the Toleration Act, allowing dissident Protestant sects to practice their religion. Their members still could not hold government office, but at least they would not be hanged. The Toleration Act did not help Catholics and Unitarians, but as is so often the case in British law, their religious practices, while not protected by formal law, were allowed by administrative discretion.

Even so, the idea of a free conscience did not advance very much; after all, "toleration" meant that a preferred or established religion, out of its own kindness, allowed other religions to exist—but not to do much more. And William's support for the Toleration Act probably had a lot to do with economic motives. Tolerance, he is supposed to have said, was essential to commercial success: England would acquire traders, including many Jews, from nations that still practiced persecution.

The Toleration Act began a slow process of moderating the political impact of organized religion. Half a century before it was passed, Galileo, tried by the Roman Inquisition for asserting that the earth moved around the sun, was sentenced to house arrest. But less than a century after the law was adopted, Adam Smith wrote a much-praised book on morality that scarcely mentioned God, and less than a century after that, Charles Darwin described the mechanisms of natural selection without reference to God; his stance profoundly disturbed his religious critics but did not prevent his books from being wildly popular or deter the Royal Society of London from bestowing on him its Royal Medal.

Toleration in the American colonies began slowly but accelerated rapidly when our country had to form a nation out of diverse states. The migration of religious sects to America made the colonies a natural breeding ground for religious freedom, but only up to a point. Though Rhode Island under the leadership of Roger Williams had become a religiously free colony, some colonies required that residents adhere to specific doctrines—belief in heaven and hell, or the Trinity, or the divine inspiration of the Bible— and some permitted only Protestants to vote. Five colonies had officially established churches. Massachusetts was a theocracy that punished (and on a few occasions executed) Quakers. Maryland was created as a haven for Catholics, but their freedom began to evaporate as Protestants slowly gained the upper hand.

America in the seventeenth and eighteenth centuries had many religions and some tolerance for dissenting views, but not until the colonists tried to form a national union did they squarely face the problem of religious freedom. In order to become a nation, the thirteen colonies had to decide how to manage the extraordinary diversity of the country. They did so largely by writing a constitution that was silent on the question of religion, except to ban any "religious test" as a requirement for holding federal office.

When the first Congress adopted the Bill of Rights, it included the odd and much-disputed ban on passing a law "respecting an establishment of religion." The meaning of that phrase is a matter of scholarly speculation. James Madison's original proposal was that the First Amendment ban "any national religion," and in their first drafts the House and Senate agreed. But when the two branches of Congress turned over their slightly different language to a conference committee, its members, for reasons that no one has satisfactorily explained, chose to ban Congress from passing a law "respecting" a religion.

The wall between church and state, as Jefferson called it in a letter he wrote many years later, turned out to be controversial and porous, as Philip Hamburger's masterful book, *The Separation of Church and State*, shows. But it did guarantee that in time American politics would largely become a secular matter. And that is the essence of the issue. Politics made it necessary to establish free consciences in America, just as it had in England. This profound change in the relationship between governance and spirituality was greatly helped by John Locke's writings in England and James Madison's in America, but I suspect it would have occurred if neither of these men had ever lived.

There is no similar story to be told in the Middle Eastern parts of the Muslim world. With the exception of Turkey (and, for a while, Lebanon), every country there has been ruled either by a radical Islamic sect (the Taliban in Afghanistan and the mullahs in Iran) or by an autocrat who uses military power to enforce his authority in a nation that cannot separate religion and politics, or by a traditional tribal chieftain, for whom the distinction between church and state is meaningless. And the failure to make a theocracy work is evident in the vast popular resistance to the Taliban and the Iranian mullahs.

It is striking that where Muslims have had to end colonial rule and build their own nation, national identity has trumped religious uniformity. When the Indonesians threw off Dutch rule and later struggled to end Communist influence, they did so in a way that made the creation and main-tenance of an Indonesian nation more important than religious or political identity. India, home to more Muslims than Egypt and Iran combined, also relied on nationalism and the overthrow of British rule to insist on the creation of one nation. Its constitution prohibits discrimination based on religion and promises the free exercise of religious belief.

But in the Middle East, nations are either of recent origin or uncertain boundaries. Iraq, once the center of great ancient civilizations, was conquered by the Mongols and the Ottoman Turks, occupied by the British during the First World War, made a League of Nations protectorate, convulsed by inter-nal wars with the Kurds, torn apart by military coups, and immersed in a long war with Iran. Syria, a land with often-changing borders, was occupied by an endless series of other powers—the Hittites, Egyptians, Assyrians, Greeks, Romans, Arabs, Mongols, Ottoman Turks, and French. After Syria became a self-governing nation in 1944, it was, like Iraq, preoccupied with a series of military coups, repeated wars with Israel, and, in 1991, war with Iraq. Meanwhile, Lebanon, once part of Syria, became an independent nation, though it later fell again under Syrian domination.

These countries today are about where England was in the eleventh century, lacking much in the way of a clear national history or stable government. To manage religion and freedom, they have yet to acquire regimes in which one set of leaders can be replaced in an orderly fashion with a new set, an accomplishment that in the West required almost a millennium. Though many Middle Eastern countries are divided between two Muslim sects, the Sunni and the Shiite, coping with this diversity has so far been vastly less important than the still-incomplete task of finding some basis for asserting and maintaining national government.

Moreover, the Muslim religion is quite different from Christianity. The Qur'an and the *hadith* contain a vast collection of sacred laws, which Muslims call *shari'a*, that regulates many details of the public as well as private lives of believers. It sets down rules governing charity, marriage, orphans, fasting, gambling, vanity, pilgrimages, infidelity, polygamy, incest, divorce, modesty, inheritances, prostitution, alcohol consumption, interest collection, and female dress.

By contrast, the Christian New Testament has rather few secular rules, and these are best remembered as a reaffirmation of the Ten Commandments as modified by the Sermon on the Mount. One can grasp the whole of the moral teachings of Jesus by recalling only two things: love God, and love your neighbor as yourself.

As Bernard Lewis has pointed out, the differences between the legal teachings of the two religions may have derived from, and were certainly reinforced by, the differences between Muhammad and Jesus. In the seventh century, Muhammad was invited to rule Medina and then, after an initial failure to conquer Mecca, finally entered that city as its ruler. He was not only a prophet but also a soldier, judge, and governor. Jesus, by contrast, was an outsider who neither conquered nor governed anyone, and who was put to death by Roman rulers. Christianity was not recognized until Emperor Constantine adopted it, but Muhammad, in Lewis's words, was his own Constantine.

Jesus asked Christians to distinguish between what belonged to God and what belonged to Caesar. Islam made no such distinction; Allah prescribed the rules for all of life, encompassing what we now call the religious and the secular spheres. If a Christian nation fails, we look to its political and economic system for an explanation, but when a Muslim state fails, Muslims believe (as V. S. Naipaul put it) that "men had failed the faith." Disaster in a

Christian nation leads to a search for a new political form; disaster in a Muslim one leads to a reinvigoration of the faith.

Christianity began as a persecuted sect, became a tolerated deviance, and then joined with political powers to become, for well over a thousand years, an official religion that persecuted its rivals. But when adhering to officially recognized religions stood in the way of maintaining successful nations, Christianity slipped back to what it had once been: an important faith without political power. And in these extraordinary changes, little in the religion was altered, because almost none of it imposed secular rules.

Judaism differs from Christianity in that it supplies its followers with a religious doctrine replete with secular rules. In the first five books of the Bible and in the Talmud, many of these rules are set forth as part of a plan, as stated in Exodus, to create "a holy nation" based on a "kingdom of priests." In the Five Books of Moses and the Talmud are rules governing slavery, diet, bribery, incest, marriage, hygiene, and crime and punishment. And many of the earliest Jewish leaders, like Muhammad later, were political and military leaders. But as Daniel Pipes has noted, for two millennia Jews had no country to rule and hence no place in which to let religion govern the state. And by the time Israel was created, the secular rules of the Old Testament and the desire to create "a holy nation" had lost their appeal to most Jews; for them, politics had simply become a matter of survival. Jews may once have been attracted to theocracy, but they had learned from experience that powerful states were dangerous ones.

Like the Old Testament, the Qur'an is hard to interpret. One can find phrases that urge Muslims to "fight and slay the pagans" and also passages that say there should be "no compulsion in religion." The Arabic word "jihad" to some means "striving in the path of God," but to others it means a holy war against infidels and apostates.

Until the rise of modern Islamic fundamentalism, many scholars sought to modernize the Qur'an by emphasizing its broadest themes more than its narrow rules. Fazlur Rahman, a leading Islamic scholar, sought in the late 1970s and early 1980s to establish a view of the Qur'an based on Muhammad's teaching that "differences among my community are a source of blessing." The basic requirement of the Qur'an, Rahman wrote, is the establishment of a social order on a moral foundation that would aim at the realization of egalitarian values. And there is much in the Qur'an to support this view: it constrained the rules permitting polygamy, moderated slavery, banned infanticide, required fair shares for wives and daughters in bequests, and allowed slaves to buy their freedom—all this in the name of the central Islamic rule: command good and forbid evil.

But many traditional Islamic scholars reject Rahman's views and insist that only the *shari'a* can govern men, even though it is impossible to manage a modern economy and sustain scientific development on the basis of principles set down in the seventh century. Bernard Lewis tells the story of a Muslim, Mirza Abu Talib, who traveled to England in the late eighteenth century. When he visited the House of Commons, he was astonished to discover that it debated and promulgated laws and set the penalties for criminals. He wrote back to his Muslim brethren that the English, not having accepted the divine law, had to make their own.

Of course, Muslim nations do legislate, but in many of them it is done furtively, with jurists describing their decisions as "customs," "regulations," or "interpretations." And in other nations, the legislature is but an amplification of the orders of a military autocrat, whose power, though often defended in religious terms, comes more from the barrel of a gun than from the teachings of the prophet.

All this makes even more remarkable the extraordinary transformation of Turkey from the headquarters of the Ottoman Empire to the place where Muslims are governed by Western law. Mustafa Kemal, now known as Atatürk, came to power after the First World War as a result of his success in helping defeat the British at Gallipoli and repelling other invading forces. For years, he had been sympathetic to the pro-Western views of many friends; when he became leader of the country, he argued that it could not duplicate the success of the West simply by buying Western arms and machines. The nation had to become Western itself.

Over the course of a decade or so, Atatürk proclaimed a new constitution, created a national legislature, abolished the sultan and caliph, required Muslims to pray in Turkish and not Arabic, urged the study of science, created a secular public education system, abolished religious courts, imposed the Latin alphabet, ended the practice of allowing divorce simply at the husband's request, gave women the vote, adopted the Christian calendar, did away with the University of Istanbul's theology faculty, created commercial legal codes by copying German and Swiss models, stated that every person was free to choose his own religion, authorized the erection of statues with human likenesses, ended the ban on alcohol (Atatürk liked to drink), converted the mosque of Hagia Sophia into a secular museum, authorized the election of the first Turkish beauty queen, and banned the wearing of the fez.

You may imagine that this last decision, part of an effort to encourage Western dress in Turkey, was a trivial matter, but you would be wrong. The fez, the red cap once worn by many Turks, conveyed social standing and, because it lacked a brim, made it possible for its wearer to touch the ground with his forehead when saying prayers. Western hats, equipped with brims, made this impossible. When the ban on the fez was announced, riots erupted in many Turkish cities, and some twenty leaders were executed.

Atatürk created the machinery (though not the fact) of democracy and made it clear that he wanted a thoroughly secular state. After his death, real democratic politics began to be practiced, as a result of which some of the anti-Islamic laws were modified. Even so, no other Middle Eastern Muslim nation has undergone as dramatic a change. In the rest of the region, autocrats still rule; they deal with religion by either buying it off or allowing it to dominate the spiritual order, provided it keeps its hands off real power.

On occasion, a fundamentalist Islamic regime comes to power, as happened in Iran, Afghanistan, and the Sudan. But these regimes have failed, ousted from Afghanistan by Western military power and declining in Iran and Sudan owing to economic incompetence and cultural rigidity.

The touchstones for Western success in reconciling religion and freedom were nationalism and Christianity, two doctrines that today many sophisticated people either ignore or distrust. But then they did not have to spend four centuries establishing freedom of conscience. We are being optimistic if we think that, absent a unique ruler such as Atatürk and a rare opportunity such as a world war, the Middle East will be able to accomplish this reconciliation much faster.

Both the West and Islam face major challenges that emerge from their ruling principles. When the West reconciled religion and freedom, it did so by making the individual the focus of society, and the price it has paid has been individualism run rampant, in the form of weak marriages, high rates of crime, and alienated personalities. When Islam kept religion at the expense of freedom, it did so by making the individual subordinate to society, and the price it has paid has been autocratic governments, religious intolerance, and little personal freedom.

I believe that in time Islam will become modern, because without religious freedom, modern government is impossible. I hope that in time the West will reaffirm social contracts, because without them a decent life is impossible. But in the near term, Islam will be on the defensive culturally—which means it will be on the offensive politically. And the West will be on the offensive culturally, which I suspect means it will be on the defensive morally.

If the Middle East is to encounter and not merely resist modernity, it would be best if it did this before it runs out of oil.

12

Islam and Freedom

Originally published in Commentary, *December 2004*

If you believe that Islamic nations can never provide freedom for their inhabitants, the world's future is dim. But it is a mistake to rely on quick generalizations. A close look at the great variety of countries where Islam is the dominant religion suggests that personal freedom, and even democratic rule, is possible under the right circumstances. Thus the long struggle to bring democracy to Iraq might not be in vain.

What are the prospects for the emergence of liberal societies in Muslim countries? Note my choice of words: "liberal," not "democratic." Democracy, defined as competitive elections among rival slates of candidates, is much harder to find in the world than liberalism, defined as a decent respect for the freedom and autonomy of individuals. There are more Muslim nations—indeed, more nations of any stripe—that provide a reasonable level of freedom than ones that provide democracy in anything like the American or British versions.

Freedom—that is, liberalism—is more important than democracy because freedom produces human opportunity. In the long run, however, democracy is essential to freedom, because no political regime will long maintain the freedoms it has provided if it keeps an ironclad grip on power. Culture and constitutions can produce freedom; democracy safeguards and expands it.

This is what lies at the heart of our efforts to make Afghanistan and Iraq into liberal states. Some on both the left and the right think it impossible to introduce democracy into the Muslim Middle East. One left-wing politician has condemned the effort as "gunpoint democracy"; a well-known leftist academic has pronounced it a "fantasy"; to a conservative journalist, open electoral systems in the Muslim world will only stimulate a competition among demagogues to see who can be the most anti-American. About Iraq specifically, the columnist George F. Will has asserted that the country lacks both democratic citizens and a democratic culture, to say nothing of lacking George Washington, James Madison, and John Marshall. Even to hope for a "liberal" regime there, he argues, is like hoping in 1917 that the socialist leader Alexander Kerensky might continue to rule Russia after Lenin and the Bolsheviks arrived.

There are certainly grounds for pessimism. Until recently, only Great Britain and its former colonies—Australia, Canada, New Zealand, and the United States—could be called democratic. And even in those countries, the struggle to acquire both liberal and democratic values was a long and hard one. It took half a millennium before England moved from the signing of Magna Carta to the achievement of parliamentary supremacy; three centuries after Magna Carta, Catholics were being burned at the stake. The United States was a British colony for two centuries, and less than a century after its independence was split by a frightful civil war. Portugal and Spain became reasonably free only late in the twentieth century, and in Latin America many societies have never even achieved the stage of liberalism. The late Daniel Patrick Moynihan once remarked that, of all the states in existence in the world in 1914, only eight would escape a violent change of government between then and the early 1990s.

Nevertheless, liberal regimes have been less uncommon than democratic ones. In 1914 there were three democracies in Europe, but many more countries where your neck would be reasonably safe from the heel of government. You might not have wished to live in Germany, but Belgium, Holland, Luxembourg, Norway, and Sweden offered reasonably attractive alternatives, even if few of them could then have been called democracies in the modern American or British sense.

As for the Middle East, there have been only three democracies in its history: Lebanon, Turkey, and of course Israel. Israel remains free and democratic despite being besieged by enemies. But of the two Muslim nations, only one, Turkey, became reasonably democratic after a fifty-year effort, while Lebanon, which has been liberal and democratic on some occasions and not on others, became a satellite of Syria and the home of anti-Israel and anti-Western terrorists. It now struggles to maintain some political distance between itself and Syria.

Is the matter as universally hopeless as this picture might suggest? Suppose, as a freedom-loving individual, you had to live in a Muslim nation somewhere in the world. You would assuredly not pick Baathist Syria or theocratic Iran. But you might pick Turkey, or Indonesia, or Morocco. In what follows, I want to explore what makes those three countries different, and what the difference might mean for the future.

Turkey is the first, the best known, and almost the only democratic secular state in the world with an overwhelmingly Muslim population. It was created in 1923 by Mustafa Kemal, later known as Atatürk, who had become a hero by expelling the Greeks from the western part of his country after World War I.

By Atatürk's time, Muslim thinkers and leaders everywhere had been struggling for centuries to find a solution to the catastrophic collapse of the Ottoman Empire. It was once the greatest empire ever known, with a remarkable record of military victories and cultural achievements to its name; but Islam was expelled from Spain in 1492, and two centuries later, the temporarily resurgent forces of the Ottomans were defeated decisively at the gates of Vienna. The Ottoman holding of Egypt had been easily captured, first by the French and then by the English.

In the early twentieth century, many who still dreamed of restoring Islam's power thought the answer lay in acquiring Western arms and Western technologies. Atatürk had a different view. It was necessary, he believed, for a Muslim nation to do more than buy Western products; it had to become Western. For him this chiefly meant turning to the principles of democracy and the teachings of science.

Speaking privately to a friend, Atatürk once remarked that "I have no religion," and that "at times I wish all religions at the bottom of the sea." Though for reasons of political prudence he allowed Turkey to be called an Islamic state, he revealed his true feelings on the matter when he converted Hagia Sofia, the great Byzantine cathedral turned Ottoman mosque, into a museum.

Atatürk favored democracy in principle but not much in practice. His followers dominated the government. Although at one point he decided there should be an opposition party, the experiment lasted only a few months before he ended it. But this is not to say that he was a dictator; instead, he was a tough ruler with a strong agenda, one who on occasion enforced that agenda by hanging dissident leaders, restricting press freedom, and crushing any organization or newspaper his government deemed subversive.

In 1945, seven years after Atatürk's death, opposition parties were again made legal in Turkey; within four years, some twenty-seven had been formed. In 1950 Turkey saw the beginnings of democratic government, with the first free elections. Thanks to Atatürk, who had made the Turkish army subservient to civilian rule, the military did nothing to prevent this development. But the army was, and has remained, determined to protect Atatürk's secularism. Whenever some leader has veered too close to a religious orientation, the Turkish military has not hesitated to intervene, each time returning to barracks once the status quo ante has been restored.

The slow emergence of democracy has, however, led to modifications in the strict antireligious stance established by Atatürk. In 1949, religious instruction was allowed on a voluntary basis. The year 2002 saw the first election of a party with a pro-Islamic leader who was not thereupon displaced by the military. This was Recep Erdogan, now Turkey's prime minister, once a follower of radical Islam and indeed jailed for inciting religious hatred. So far, though, the path of "enlightened moderation" seems to be paying dividends.

Next, Indonesia. It has taken a half century for this historically tolerant nation to move from independence, acquired in 1949, to free presidential elections, carried out earlier this year. Indonesia's first president, Sukarno, established a regime called "guided democracy," which consisted mostly of guidance with very little democracy; in 1963, he proclaimed himself president for life. Thanks to economic mismanagement, however, combined with a rapid increase in the size and influence of the Indonesian Communist Party and a disastrous decision to withdraw from the United Nations, he quickly began to wear out his welcome. In response to an attempted Communist coup d'etat in 1965, the Indonesian military removed Sukarno from power and put down the revolt in a campaign that killed hundreds of thousands.

Sukarno's successor was General Suharto, head of the military, who was repeatedly reelected to office by a large "consultative assembly" packed with handpicked supporters. To ensure his reelection, Suharto banned most political parties. Although helping to redirect the Indonesian economy—by the early 1990s, it was growing at a rate of 7 percent per year—Suharto practiced a crony capitalism that could not survive. When a severe financial crisis hit the country in 1997, he was forced to resign in favor of his vice president, who proceeded, rather surprisingly, to liberalize Indonesian politics. Scores of new political parties were created, a new election law was promulgated, civil servants and active military officers were banned from campaigning, strict limits were enacted on campaign contributions, and the presidency was limited to two five-year terms.

In the 1999 election, one major contending party was headed by Abdurrahman Wahid (popularly known as Gus Dur), the leader of a vast Muslim social organization and a moderate who favored a government without religious leanings. Another was headed by Megawati Sukarnoputri, or Mega, as she is known, the daughter of ex-president Sukarno. She, too, supported a secular state with a democratic orientation. The consultative assembly picked Wahid for the presidency; Mega, whose party won more seats in parliament than any other, became his vice president.

Frail and blind, beset by financial scandals, ethnic violence, and a weak economy, Wahid was impeached by the legislature; his place was taken by Mega, who found herself confronted by the need to deal with ethnic separatism, massive political corruption, and a moribund economy. She had only limited success. Jihad extremists, though lacking political power, became violent in Indonesia, in one case killing hundreds of civilians; and radical Islamic schools, akin to the *madrassas* of Pakistan, now number well over ten thousand. Corruption is rampant.

Under Mega, as under her predecessor, the Indonesians had one great advantage: they could remove her from office. This year there were new elections. In the first round—for parliament—Mega's party lost support in a vigorous contest with many other parties; in the subsequent balloting for a new president, Susilio Bambang Yudhoyno, a former general who once headed the security services, won decisively, the first time a sitting Indonesian president has been replaced by means of a popular vote. The new president has promised pluralism, tolerance, and a vigorous program of economic revitalization. One can only hope for the best.

Turkey and Indonesia are Muslim nations but not Arab nations. Morocco is both Muslim and Arab. After many centuries during which authority had been vested chiefly in tribal leaders, and another forty-four years as a French protectorate, Morocco became a self-governing nation in 1956. King Muhammad V, who took undisputed power with the end of French influence, received the full support of local Islamic leaders; his son King Hassan II, who assumed office in 1961, made it clear that he spoke for all of Islam, proclaiming himself a direct descendant of the Prophet Muhammad.

Thereafter, and until his death in 1999, Hassan, a playboy who had been predicted to last all of six months on the throne, played a powerful role, surviving two army plots, a left-wing revolution, the opposition of radical Muslim fundamentalists, and the hostility of Algeria and Libya. Internal turmoil did not diminish Hassan's commitment to religious liberty. Though Islam is the national religion, proselytizing was forbidden, Morocco's large Jewish population was protected, and nothing like the reactionary Wahhabi sect of Saudi Arabia was allowed to take root within the country's borders. Unlike Turkey, Morocco has never established formal diplomatic ties with Israel, but the king conferred in secret with Israeli leaders in the 1970s and welcomed Israeli prime minister Shimon Peres to Rabat in 1986.

Hassan tried to give his monarchy a legitimate basis by means of what he called "Hassanian democracy." Various draft constitutions were put to a vote, each receiving the somewhat suspicious support of well over 90 percent of the population; each authorized personal freedom and parliamentary rule while also granting the king the right to rule by decree in an emergency. One law threatened criminal prosecution for anyone publishing anything the king deemed personally offensive.

Despite these restrictions, domestic security improved, the status of women was enhanced, and radical Muslim fundamentalists were contained. The king once remarked that "true Islam is tolerant" because "tolerance is the touchstone of civilization." In the 1990s political freedoms were expanded as Hassan sought membership in the European Union. A fifth constitution, approved in 1996, led to generally free elections, with no party winning a clear majority.

Upon Hassan's death, his son assumed the throne as Muhammad VI. Announcing that he supported economic liberalism, human rights, and individual freedom, the new ruler backed up his words by granting amnesty to thousands of prisoners and overseeing elections in 2002 that were generally regarded as free and fair. Morocco has been closely attached to the West. It is formally associated with the European Union. It was the first Arab state to condemn Iraq's invasion of Kuwait. Freedom House calls today's Morocco "partly free," ranking it ahead of its neighboring Arab states of Algeria and Tunisia and just behind Indonesia and Turkey. In freedom of the press, Morocco scores well above its neighbors. A recent survey of the status of women finds their position greatly improved, with women serving in parliament and holding an increasing share of jobs.

The country is not, however, without problems. The 2002 elections created a governing coalition consisting of socialist and conservative parties and, troublingly, an opposition led by an Islamist party. In 2003, Islamic radicals carried out suicide bombings in the city of Casablanca. (The king responded that his country would "never accept that Islam" can be used "for the satisfaction of ambitions [to] rule in the name of religion.") But Morocco's greatest problem is similar to that of almost all Muslim nations: how to create economic growth.

There are other Muslim or Muslim-dominated countries, including Mali and Senegal, that show some respect for individual liberty. Kuwait has improved personal freedom since it was liberated from Iraqi rule. Even Pakistan has expanded press freedom, so that today it ranks, in the opinion of those who survey these matters, only slightly behind India.

What general conclusions can we draw from this brief survey? The first element that most of the freer Muslim countries have in common is the effort to detach religion from politics. This they have done by being secular (Turkey), by constraining Islamic leaders (Indonesia), or by having a ruler who combines religious tradition with secular rule (Morocco).

To do any of these things, one needs a powerful and decisive leader. No one reading accounts of Atatürk and Hassan can fail to acknowledge the force of their personalities and the enduring loyalties they managed to command. So deeply did Sukarno implant the commitment to Indonesian nationalism as a key ingredient of his regime that his successor Suharto continued to embrace the same secular national ideology, complete with its emphasis on unity and religious tolerance. For years, any Indonesian political party, including religious ones, had to endorse this doctrine (called *Pancasila*) or risk being banned.

Separating religion from politics was the key to the development of liberal nations in the West, and it will be the key to the emergence of such states in the Muslim world. To date, however, the autocratic rulers of the Muslim Middle East have either installed theocratic leaders (Iran, the Taliban), or suppressed religious dissent without allowing political freedom (Egypt, Syria), or done both (Saudi Arabia).

Many people wonder whether, in this respect, Arab states differ essentially from non-Arab Muslim states. It is a good question, but I do not think we know the answer. Even what constitutes an "Arab state" is a bit ambiguous. A country can be called Arab if its people speak Arabic or are descended from inhabitants of the Arabian peninsula, or if its government is part of the Arab League. Twenty-four countries have Arabic as their official language. Among them are Morocco, which has made substantial progress toward liberalization, and Bahrain and Kuwait, which have made a bit of progress. These are, admittedly, more than matched by the autocratic regimes we find in Egypt, Libya, Sudan, Syria, and Saudi Arabia. But the picture among non-Arab Muslim states is mixed as well: although Indonesia and Turkey have become reasonably free, against them one must set the mullah-controlled regime in non-Arab Iran.

Another conclusion about Islam and liberalism concerns the role of the military. In nations with strong but not autocratic rulers (Turkey, Indonesia), the army has stood decisively for secular rule and opposed efforts to create an Islamist state; when fundamentalist parties arise, the military has usually shut them down, sometimes imprisoning their leaders. In a place like Pakistan, by contrast, the military has been divided and has on occasion supported Islamic claims; the same goes for Morocco, where the military has sometimes launched ill-conceived attacks on King Hassan but at other times waged a successful battle against rebels in the Western Sahara supported by neighboring Algeria.

The tolerably liberal regimes have enjoyed still other advantages. For one thing, none of them has had to struggle against a significant ethnic minority demanding independence. Indonesia is overwhelmingly Muslim (except on Bali, a Hindu island known not for any desire for independence but for its happy inwardness). There are Kurds in Turkey with separatist views, but with the exception of a violent fringe they have not challenged the sovereignty of Ankara. In Morocco, some see a difference between Arabs and tribal Berbers; over the last decades, however, this difference has produced few major political quarrels.

In none of these three countries, moreover, are there significant conflicts between Sunni and Shiite Muslims—for the simple reason that there are virtually no Shiites to be found in them. This offers a striking contrast to, say, Iraq and Pakistan.

Finally, it is important to note the continuing impact of the West on Muslim political systems, both for good and for ill. Socialism was embraced by Sukarno in Indonesia, which led to economic chaos and his replacement by Suharto. Fascism has been the basis of the Baath parties in Syria and Iraq, and in the latter it provided the basis for the quarter-century rule of Saddam Hussein. Another Western idea, liberal democracy, became rooted in Turkey, though it took over a half-century to do so.

But in most Muslim countries today, the chief rival to autocratic secular rule has been not Western ideologies but Islam. On a purely institutional level, it is not hard to see why. Islam is organized into mosques, and many of these support charitable and educational organizations that provide services reaching deep into the society. Political activism gathers around religion the way salt crystallizes along a string dangling in seawater.

The Protestant Reformation helped set the stage for religious and even political freedom in the West. Can something like it occur in Muslim nations? That is highly doubtful. Islam offers neither a papacy nor a priesthood against which to rebel; nor does it dispense sacraments, as the Catholic Church does. There will never be a Muslim Martin Luther or a hereditary Islamic ruler who, by embracing a new or rival faith, can thereby create an opportunity for lay rule.

Thus, although there are moderate Islamic leaders, the best-known voices are those of the radicals, who use language ominously resembling that of Ayatollah Khomeini, the revolutionary who captured Iran from the Shah. Abdessalam Yassine, described by some as the major Moroccan political alternative to King Muhammad VI, wants to create an "Islamic democracy" in which governance would be entrusted to "the wise, not the sly." Rachid Ghannouchi, an exiled Tunisian leader, says he hopes somehow to preserve the Muslim faith while allowing personal freedom. But Ghannouchi also decries the Western freedom that has produced "greed, deception, and brutality" and that believes in no "absolute value that transcends the will of man." To him, a free man should be "God's vice-regent." Many religiously inspired Westerners might agree with this in a metaphoric sense, but the historical lesson of the liberal West is that freedom trumps absolute values. This fact creates a problem Ghannouchi cannot solve.

As I have noted, political freedom in the West emerged out of a centuries-long struggle between the church and its religious opponents. Tolerance slowly emerged as the only feasible alternative to intrareligious conflict. After many centuries, such religious tolerance was converted into secular rule in England, France, Germany, and Scandinavia. It may therefore take a long time before the proponents of "Islamic democracy," whatever that slippery term means, abandon their efforts and realize that no nation can be governed effectively simply on the basis of Islamic law.

How does all this relate to Iraq? Like Jordan, Lebanon, and Syria, Iraq was created by European mapmakers after World War I. The borders of the new nation corresponded somewhat to those of Mesopotamia, a region once called the cradle of civilization. But when Iraq was created, as Margaret MacMillan points out in *Paris 1919*, a history of mapmaking after World War I, "there was no Iraqi people." There was also "no Iraqi nationalism, only Arab." The population was deeply divided, with Basra oriented toward India, Baghdad toward Persia, and Mosul toward Turkey. Creating one nation in that place was akin to creating Yugoslavia after World War II. It could only be done by a powerful ruler, like Tito.

Great Britain tried twice to bring strong central government to Iraq, and both times it failed. In the 1920s the British army occupied the country; when that became too costly, the British withdrew, leaving behind a constitution that empowered King Faisal. When Faisal died and his son could not manage affairs, the country splintered along ethnic lines. Civil war erupted, with military officers emerging as heroes. By the 1930s, the army controlled politics.

At the beginning of World War II the British Army once again occupied Iraq, in order to prevent Baghdad from forming an alliance with Adolf Hitler that would have jeopardized access to Iraqi oil. Britain also wanted to prevent the creation of an anti-British barrier between Egypt and India. This time the army stayed for seven years, ending with a failed effort to create a constitutional monarchy. As soon as its troops departed, the Iraqi army took power and initiated a reign that did not end until the American invasion in 2003.

Our chances of leaving an enduring legacy of freedom in Iraq are therefore uncertain. But uncertain does not mean impossible. An opinion poll taken in April 2004 suggests that, at least in principle, the Iraqi people do support liberal and democratic government. About 40 percent want a multiparty democracy like that found in most European nations, while only about 13 percent say they would prefer a theocracy of the sort found in Iran. The success of the military tactics instituted by General Petraeus has allowed the civilian government to become much stronger and its army to make the country safer. But no one will know how lasting these changes will be until the country must change its leaders peaceably.

To be sure, support for a parliamentary democracy is unevenly distributed. Those who live in heavily Shiite areas are about as likely to want a theocracy as a democracy, while in the Sunni areas, where our troops have experienced the most attacks, and where the once-dominant but heavily outnumbered Sunnis fear majority-Shiite rule, a parliamentary system is the most popular choice.

The good news is that, as compared with support for democracy, support for a *liberal* regime is very broad. Over 90 percent want free speech, about three-fourths want freedom of religion, and over three-fourths favor free assembly. Freedom is more important than democracy—a fact that might well have been true in America and England in the eighteenth century.

And here is where an important lesson lurks for us. Scholars at the RAND Corporation have studied America's efforts at nation building in the last half century, ranging from our successes (Germany and Japan) to our failures (Haiti and Somalia) and to all the uncertain outcomes in between (Afghanistan, Bosnia, Kosovo). One of the most important things we should have learned, they conclude, is that "while staying long does not guarantee success, leaving early ensures failure."

In order for freedom to have a chance of developing in Iraq, we must be patient as well as strong. It would be an unmitigated disaster to leave too early—it would crush our Iraqi supporters, hand victory to terrorists and Islamic radicals, and mean that our own struggle and sacrifices were for naught.

Liberalism and democracy would bring immeasurable gains to Iraq, and through Iraq to the Middle East as a whole. So far, the country lacks what has helped other Muslim nations make the change—a remarkably skilled and powerful leader, a strong army devoted to secular rule, and an absence of ethnic conflict. If I remain nevertheless cautiously optimistic, it is because of the hope that we will indeed stay there as long as we are needed.

13

Democracy for All?

Originally published in Commentary, *March 2000*

Democracy is hard to achieve and difficult to preserve. It took centuries to develop out of its English roots and now faces new problems with the increase in the number of Muslims in Europe. And China is the greatest puzzle: will it follow its extraordinary success in creating a vibrant economy by embracing a democratic polity? I have no idea what the future holds but offer in this essay some under-standing of how we got where we are.

∞∞∞

Today we wonder whether the whole world might become democratic. Acting on the belief that it can, our government has bent its energies toward encouraging the birth or growth of democracy in places around the globe from Haiti to Russia, from Kosovo to the People's Republic of China. In doing so, it has enjoyed a kind of sanction from the century just past, which was indeed marked by the growth of regimes resting on popular consent and a commitment to human freedom.

That was hardly the only salient characteristic of the age; the twentieth century was also an era of mass murder, in which more than 170 million people were killed by their own governments. In some ways, in fact, it is easier to explain that phenomenon than to explain the increase in the number of democratic regimes. Living for most of their history in tiny villages, people have customarily viewed those in other villages as at best distant strangers and at worst mortal enemies. When agriculture and industry brought people together into large cities, the stage was set for dictatorial leaders, driven by power and ideology and aided by modern technology, to seize and maintain political control by destroying not only

165

their personal rivals but entire populations who could be depicted as the enemies of the state. In the worst cases, this destruction has amounted to genocide.

But if hostility and mass murder can, alas, be easily explained, democracy is an oddity. How do people who evolved in small, homogeneous villages become tolerant of those whom they do not know and who may differ from them in habits and religion? How can village government, based on tradition and consensus, be transformed into national government based on votes cast by strangers?

Democratic government cannot rest simply on written constitutions. Many Latin American nations have had constitutions similar to that of the United States but have practiced not democracy but oligarchy. Religion may help foster tolerance, if people take the Golden Rule seriously. But we know that some religious people are fanatics and some agnostics tolerant. We also know that in some faiths, such as Islam, there is no separation between religious and secular law, and that the absence of this distinction tempts religious leaders to impose authoritarian rule on their followers. Voltaire once said that a nation with one church will have oppression; with two, civil war; with a hundred, freedom. Religious freedom strengthens political freedom, but religious freedom exists only after political freedom has been secured.

In what follows I do not intend to dwell on the ideas that have inspired, shaped, and informed democratic government. Rather, I want to suggest some conditions that to my mind have underlain the emergence and survival of our oldest democracies. They come under four headings.

The first is *isolation*. The freest nations have been protected from invasion by broad oceans or high mountains. England, Australia, New Zealand, and the United States enjoy ocean boundaries; Switzerland has a mountainous one. The significance of isolation is that it minimizes the need for a large standing army commanded by a single ruler, thus minimizing the need for high taxes to sustain the army and unfettered authority to empower the ruler. By contrast, in nations without secure boundaries— France, Austria, Hungary, Prussia—demands for popular rule and for a weak central government had to be subordinated to the need for a powerful army.

Imagine what life in the United States would have been like if Spain had remained in Florida and France had retained the Louisiana territory. To manage the inevitable skirmishes and wars, our national government would have grown more powerful more quickly and would have taxed and regulated more heavily.

The second condition is *property*. For many modern thinkers, private property is the enemy of human equality and therefore of democracy. Property is theft, wrote Proudhon. The *Communist Manifesto* promised the abolition of private property, and generations of social planners have sought to diminish its reach. But in fact private property is the friend of democracy. Aristotle understood that it stimulates work by providing rewards to the owner, reduces arguments by supplying a basis for allocating goods, and enhances pleasure by creating a physical object for human affection. In his *Politics* he first describes the private household and how it is managed before going on to argue that government exists to perfect the character of the householders.

But private property furthers democracy only if ownership is widespread. If one rich man has almost all the property and many poor men have none, a struggle will ensue between the landowner and the landless. A central question, therefore, is which historical forces produce the widespread ownership of property and which do not. To this question, Alan MacFarlane of Cambridge University has given powerful answers in *The Origins of English Individualism* (1978).

In much of medieval Europe outside England, land was owned by clans or extended families, which managed their land collectively. Farms produced goods chiefly for families rather than for markets, and, as children were required to run the farm, marriages were arranged at an early age for the convenience of the clan.

Since clan control of property meant that land rarely changed hands, hardly any law was created to govern such transactions. Since farm produce was seldom sold, little law was developed to govern exchanges. Since marriages were arranged, there was little law to govern conjugal matters. In short, little law was developed of the sort we now recognize. And, with little law, few courts were needed to interpret or apply it. Such tribunals as existed were not independent of other sources of authority; their rulings reflected the personal decision or will of the feudal prince.

In England and perhaps elsewhere in northwestern Europe, MacFarlane shows, matters were very different. From at least the thirteenth century on, individual ownership of land was common. Though parents exercised a great deal of authority over their households, and thus over their land, they did not do so as representatives of a clan that collectively controlled it. Land could be bought, sold, bequeathed, and inherited. Many people were poor, but most were not landless.

Individual ownership was so important in England that a man had to own land before starting a family. Since it might take a long time for this to happen, marriages occurred later in life than was the case in Eastern Europe. In England, too, the prospective husband and wife usually had to agree to the union, including one arranged by their parents. Many married over parental objections.

Because land in England could change hands easily, a body of rulings grew up to manage such transactions. This collection of individual decisions, later accepted and codified by others, became the common law of England. It was produced by courts that to a large degree were independent of the king, and it contained judgments independent of his authority. The legal claims granted by this law constituted a set of rights—not broad rights aimed at political power but rights of ownership, sale, and title. Once the language of rights entered public consciousness, however, it was only a matter of time before these selfsame rights, interpreted and applied by the independent courts, became claims against the king.[1]

Just why England and a few other nations of northwestern Europe took this path of individual property rights and helped create a property-oriented legal system is not well understood. But having taken that path, they also laid the groundwork for democratic rule that was to come several centuries later—groundwork that was then exported to America, English Canada, Australia, and New Zealand.

The third condition is *homogeneity*. During the cold war we could be excused for thinking that the great drivers of human life were ideology and economics. In fact, however, as Daniel P. Moynihan has observed, the deepest and most pervasive source of human conflict is ethnic rivalry. Russia has broken apart on ethnic lines; much of Africa and the Middle East is split along ethnic lines; Yugoslavia has sundered on ethnic lines. World War I was a struggle over "national"—that is, ethnic—self-determination, and World War II, though it might have been waged by Hitler under any circumstances, was justified by him in the name of the alleged superiority of "Aryans" and their presumed right to be politically reunited with their fellow "Aryans" in other nations.

Several democratic nations are today ethnically diverse, but at the time democracy was being established, that diversity was so limited that it could be safely ignored. England was an Anglo-Saxon nation; America, during its founding period, was overwhelmingly English; so also, by and large, were Australia, Canada, and New Zealand.

Then there is Switzerland—ethnically quite a diverse society that nonetheless managed to create a democracy out of an alliance among French, German, and Italian speakers who were divided almost equally between Protestants and Catholics. The Swiss model—a democratic nation in which much authority, especially that of the courts, is left in the hands of the cantons and only modest powers are bequeathed to the national president—is a fascinating one, but so far it has hardly served as a guide to other nations.

I am not suggesting that ethnic homogeneity is a good thing or ought to be preserved at any cost; nor am I denying that democracies can become ethnically heterogeneous. Certainly one of the great glories of the United States is to have become both vigorously democratic and ethnically diverse. But it is a rare accomplishment. Historically, and with few exceptions, the growth of democracy and of respect for human rights occurred more easily—often much more easily—in nations that had a more or less common culture.

Indeed, in the formative years of a nation, ethnic diversity can be as great a problem as foreign enemies. The time, power, and money that must be devoted to maintaining one ethnic group in power is at least equivalent to the resources needed to protect against a foreign enemy. When one part of a people thinks another part is unworthy of rights, it is hard for a government to act in the name of the "rights of the people." That is why democracy in England preceded democracy in the United Kingdom: because many parts of that kingdom—the Scots, the Irish—had very different views about who should rule them and how. They still do.

Finally, *tradition*. Democratic politics is rarely produced overnight. In 1914, Europe had only three democracies. By the end of World War I, that number had grown to thirteen; but by the time of the next war, the number had fallen again as Germany, Italy, and other nations became authoritarian.

Between 1950 and 1990, there were roughly as many authoritarian regimes as democratic ones, and the rate at which democratic regimes changed into authoritarian ones was about the same as the rate at which authoritarian systems changed into democratic ones.

The oldest democracy, England, relied heavily on a tradition of human rights to move slowly toward modern democratic rule. Its problem—one that every nation must eventually face, and usually over a much briefer period—was how to get a government to respect the rights of people who did not necessarily support it. In this connection, the great event in English history was the signing of Magna Carta in 1215.

Magna Carta hardly resembled the American Bill of Rights. It was not a constitution or part of a constitution; much of it concerned taxes, debts, fines, licenses, and inheritances. Except for a few passages about not delaying or denying justice and not imprisoning people save by the judgment of their peers, it had little to do with human rights, let alone modern government.

But as the late Erwin Griswold of the Harvard Law School once put it, "Magna Carta is not primarily significant for what it was, but rather for what it came to be." Five centuries after it was written, it had become the touchstone for English liberties.

How so? Because it was constantly invoked whenever the king was at odds with his barons or his people. On at least forty occasions over several centuries, the document was confirmed by the king, usually as a way of settling some current grievance; and every time the king restated his loyalty to it, Magna Carta gained authority. When the Puritan revolutionaries came to power, they did so in part in order to restore Magna Carta, a document most of them had probably never read.

As it passed into English folklore, so also was it exported to America. American colonists spoke of having "the rights of Englishmen," by which they meant the rights specified in Magna Carta and the subsequent decisions allegedly justified by it. Andrew Hamilton defended Peter Zenger's right to publish freely by reference to Magna Carta, even though the document says nothing about free speech. The constitutions of the United States and of several individual states put into writing the assumptions of Magna Carta: government has limited and defined powers, the judiciary should be independent, private property is important, and the "law of the land"—that is, British common law—should be the basis for settling disputes.

In America, the Declaration of Independence acquired a power similar to that of Magna Carta, but this time for reasons that could be more easily discerned in the text, with its "self-evident" truths that all men are entitled to life, liberty, and "the pursuit of happiness," and its assertion that these entitlements can be abridged only by due process of law. The Declaration and the Bill of Rights have become icons of American politics, to which people instantly give loyalty even though they may in practice disagree with one or more of their provisions.

For an illustration, finally, of the crucial importance of democratic tradition, we need only look to Japan. It is geographically isolated, its people own property, and it is ethnically homogeneous. But until 1945 it lacked any strong tradition of personal liberty and democratic rule. And so democracy came late to Japan, and at the point of a bayonet.

Will, then, the whole world become democratic? Unless history offers no lessons at all, one must have doubts. None of the conditions I have mentioned—isolation, private property, ethnic homogeneity, and deeply felt traditions of human rights—can be found in China or Russia or in much of Africa or the Middle East. Bits and pieces exist in parts of Latin America, more so lately than earlier, but that region's welcome flirtation with democratic rule is still relatively short-lived.

There are two ways democracy can spread despite the absence of the historical forces that have produced it elsewhere. One is through military conquest. In the twentieth century, English rule provided the basis for democracy in India, just as in the twentieth century the victorious Allies provided it for Germany and, as I have noted, Japan. In all three cases, nations having little experience with democracy had its lessons forcibly imposed, and so successfully that it has survived and shows every sign of entrenchment. But since democracies rarely conquer other nations, this mechanism will seldom be available.

The other way is economic globalization. Not every nation with free markets is democratic, but every democratic nation has something akin to a free market. Free markets both foster and require an openness to new ideas and scientific inquiry, opportunity for innovation, and a prudent level of regulation—attributes hard to come by in undemocratic regimes. The arrival of globalization and the Internet are making it clear to everybody in every nation just where one can buy the best goods at the lowest prices. In the face of widespread knowledge about what efficiency can achieve, non-democratic governments will have to scramble to maintain inefficiency.

Of course, scramble they will. Singapore believes that it can be both prosperous and undemocratic, and so far it has managed. China has bet that it can do the same. But will these successes endure? No one can be certain. An optimistic friend of mine has predicted that, because it wishes to be rich, China will become democratic by the year 2013. Perhaps. My question is whether it will still be democratic in the year 2033.

In the long run, democracy and human freedom are good for everyone even though they may create some mischief in the near term. But the good they bring can be appreciated only when people are calm and tolerance is accepted. The late Edward C. Banfield, perhaps the best student of American politics in modern times, said something about political systems in general that applies with particular force to democracies:

> A political system is an accident. It is an accumulation of habits, customs, prejudices, and principles that have survived a long process of trial and error and of ceaseless response to changing circumstances. If the system works well on the whole, it is a lucky accident—the luckiest, indeed, that can befall a society, for all of the institutions of the society, and thus its entire character and that of the human types formed within it, depend ultimately on the government and the political order.

To this I would add that a workable democracy is the happiest accident of all. By nurturing ours, we may perhaps hope that others will acquire something equally worthy of nurturance.

Note

1. There was, of course, a landowning English aristocracy, but an aristocrat's status was not defined by any legal claim applying to him as an individual. According to the English rule of primogeniture, only the eldest son inherited the land and hence the title, while other sons had neither a claim on the land nor membership in the aristocracy. They might be wealthy because of gifts from their father, but they were not dukes because he was a duke. In France, by contrast, where there was no primogeniture, every son of a duke had a share in his father's land and a claim on an aristocratic title. The kings of France thus had to devote a great deal of time to managing their large, unwieldy, and rivalrous aristocracy.

PART III

Heredity and Politics

14

The DNA of Politics: Genes Shape Our Beliefs, Our Values, and Even Our Votes

Originally published in City Journal, *Winter 2009*

I am a social scientist, which should imply that I believe that social forces shape human nature. But biology has shown that this view is no longer credible: our genetic endowment has extraordinary influence over not only who we are but what we believe. And though nurture plays an important role, its influence is not chiefly wielded by what we once supposed was nurture's greatest influence: the family.

Children differ, as any parent of two or more knows. Some babies sleep through the night, others are always awake; some are calm, others are fussy; some walk at an early age, others after a long wait. Scientists have proved that genes are responsible for these early differences. But people assume that as children get older and spend more time under their parents' influence, the effect of genes declines. They are wrong.

For a century or more, we have understood that intelligence is largely inherited, though even today some mistakenly rail against the idea and say that nurture, not nature, is all. Now we know that much of our personality, too, is inherited, and that there is some genetic basis for some psychiatric illnesses and many social attitudes and behaviors, including our involvement in crime. Some things do result entirely from environmental influences, such as whether you follow the Red Sox or the Yankees (though I suspect that Yankee fans have a genetic defect). But beyond routine tastes, almost everything has some genetic basis. And that includes politics.

When scholars say that a trait is "inherited," they don't mean that they can tell what role nature and nurture have played in any given individual. Rather, they mean that in a population—say, a group of adults or children—genes explain a lot of the differences among individuals.

There are two common ways of reaching this conclusion. One is to compare adopted children's traits with those of their biological parents, on the one hand, and with those of their adoptive parents, on the other. If a closer correlation exists with the biological parents' traits, then we say that the trait is to that degree inherited.

The other method is to compare identical twins' similarity, with respect to some trait, with the similarity of fraternal twins, or even of two ordinary siblings. Identical twins are genetic duplicates, while fraternal twins share only about half their genes and are no more genetically alike than ordinary siblings are. If identical twins are more alike than fraternal twins, therefore, we conclude that the trait under consideration is to some degree inherited.

Three political science professors—John Alford, Carolyn Funk, and John Hibbing—have studied political attitudes among a large number of twins in America and Australia. They measured the attitudes with something called the Wilson-Patterson Scale (I am not the Wilson after whom it was named), which asks whether a respondent agrees or disagrees with twenty-eight words or phrases, such as "death penalty," "school prayer," "pacifism," or "gay rights." They then compared the similarity of the responses among identical twins with the similarity among fraternal twins. They found that, for all twenty-eight taken together, the identical twins did indeed agree with each other more often than the fraternal ones did—and that genes accounted for about 40 percent of the difference between the two groups. On the other hand, the answers these people gave to the words "Democrat" or "Republican" had a very weak genetic basis. In politics, genes help us understand fundamental attitudes—that is, whether we are liberal or conservative—but do not explain what party we choose to join.

Genes also influence how frequently we vote. Voting has always puzzled scholars: how is it rational to wait in line on a cold November afternoon when there is almost no chance that your ballot will make any difference? Apparently, people who vote often feel a strong sense of civic duty or like to express themselves. But who are these people? James Fowler, Laura Baker, and Christopher Dawes studied political participation in Los Angeles by comparing voting among identical and fraternal twins. Their conclusion: among registered voters, genetic factors explain about 60 percent of the difference between those who vote and those who do not.

A few scholars, determined to hang on to the belief that environment explains everything, argue that such similarities occur because the parents of identical twins—as opposed to the parents of fraternal twins—encourage them to be as alike as possible as they grow up. This is doubtful. First, we know that many parents make bad guesses about their children's genetic connection—thinking that fraternal twins are actually identical ones, or vice versa. When we take twins' accurate genetic relationships into account, we find that identical twins whom parents wrongly thought to be fraternal are very similar, while fraternal twins wrongly thought to be identical are no more alike than ordinary siblings.

Moreover, studying identical twins reared apart by different families effectively shows that their similar traits cannot be the result of similar upbringing. The University of Minnesota's Thomas Bouchard has done research on many identical twins reared apart (some in different countries) and has found that though they never knew each other or their parents, they proved remarkably alike, especially in personality—whether they were extroverted, agreeable, neurotic, or conscientious, for example.

Some critics complain that the fact that identical twins live together with their birth parents, at least for a time, ruins Bouchard's findings: during this early period, they say, parenting must influence the children's attitudes. But the average age at which the identical twins in Bouchard's study became separated from their parents was five months. It is hard to imagine parents teaching five-month-old babies much about politics or religion.

The gene-driven ideological split that Alford and his colleagues found may, in fact, be an underestimate, because men and women tend to marry people with whom they agree on big issues—assortative mating, as social scientists call it. Assortative mating means that the children of parents who agree on issues will be more likely to share whatever genes influence those beliefs. Thus, even children who are not identical twins will have a larger genetic basis for their views than if their parents married someone with whom they disagreed. Since we measure heritability by subtracting the similarity among fraternal twins from the similarity among identical ones, this difference may neglect genetic influences on fraternal twins that already exist. And if it does, it means that we are underestimating genetic influences on attitudes.

When we step back and look at American politics generally, genes may help us understand why, for countless decades, about 40 percent of all voters have supported conservative causes, about 40 percent have backed liberal ones, and the 20 percent in the middle have decided the elections. On a few occasions, the winning presidential candidate has won about 60 percent of the vote. But these days we call a 55 percent victory a "landslide." It is hard to imagine a purely environmental force that would rule out a presidential election in which one candidate got 80 percent of the vote and his rival only 20 percent. Something deeper must be going on.

All of this leaves open the question: which genes help create which political attitudes? Right now, we don't know. To discover the links will require lengthy studies of the DNA of people with different political views. Scientists are having a hard time locating the specific genes that cause diseases; it will probably be much harder to find the complex array of genes that affects politics.

Of course, there are problems with the observed link between genes and politics. One is that it is fairly crude so far. Liberals and conservatives come in many varieties: one can be an economic liberal and a social conservative, say, favoring a large state but opposing abortion; or an economic conservative and a social liberal, favoring the free market but supporting abortion and gay rights. If we add attitudes about foreign policy to the mix, the combinations double. Most tests used in genetic studies of political views do not allow us to make these important distinctions. As a result, though we know that genes affect ideology, that knowledge is still very rough. In time, I suspect, we will be able to refine it.

Further, it's important to emphasize that biology is not destiny. Genetic influences rarely operate independently of environmental factors. Take the case of serotonin. People who have little of this neurotransmitter are at risk for some psychological problems, but for many of them, no such problems occur unless they experience some personal crisis. Then the combined effect of genetic influences and disruptive experiences will trigger a deep state of depression, something that does not happen to people who either do not lack serotonin or do lack it but encounter no crisis. Recently, in the first study to find some of the exact genes that affect political participation,

Fowler and Dawes found two genes that help explain voting behavior. One of the genes, influencing serotonin levels, boosts turnout by 10 percent—if the person also attends church frequently. Nature and nurture interact.

The same is probably true of political ideology. When campus protests and attacks on university administrators began in the late 1960s, it was not because a biological upheaval had increased the number of radicals; it was because such people encountered events (the war in Vietnam, the struggle over civil rights) and group pressures that induced them to take strong actions. By the same token, lynchings in the South did not become common because there were suddenly more ultra-racists around. Rather, mob scenes, media frenzies, and the shock of criminal events motivated people already skeptical of civil rights to do terrible things.

Another challenge is politicized assessment of the genetic evidence. Ever since 1950, when Theodor Adorno and his colleagues published *The Authoritarian Personality*, scholars have studied right-wing authoritarianism but neglected its counterpart on the left. In his study of identical twins reared apart, Bouchard concludes that right-wing authoritarianism is, to a large degree, inherited—but he says nothing about authoritarianism on the left. This omission is puzzling, since as Bouchard was studying twins at the University of Minnesota, he was regularly attacked by left-wing students outraged by the idea that any traits might be inherited. A few students even threatened to kill him. When I pointed this out to him, he suggested, in good humor, that I was a troublemaker.

Yet if you ask who in this country has prevented people from speaking on college campuses, it is overwhelmingly leftists. If you ask who storms the streets and shatters the windows of Starbucks coffee shops to protest the World Trade Organization, it is overwhelmingly leftists. If you ask who produces campus codes that infringe on free speech, it is overwhelmingly leftists. If you ask who invaded the classroom of my late colleague Richard Herrnstein and tried to prevent him from teaching, it was overwhelmingly leftists.

A better way to determine if authoritarianism is genetic would be to ask people what the country's biggest problems are. Liberals might say the inequality of income or the danger of global warming; conservatives might indicate the tolerance of abortion or the abundance of pornography. You would then ask each group what they thought should be done to solve these problems. An authoritarian liberal might say that we should tax high incomes out of existence and close down factories that emit greenhouse gases. A conservative authoritarian might suggest that we put abortion doctors in jail and censor books and television programs. This approach would give us a true measure of authoritarians, left and right, and we would know how many of each kind existed and something about their backgrounds. Then, if they had twins, we would be able to estimate the heritability of authoritarianism. Doing all this is a hard job, which may explain why no scholars have done it.

Genes shape, to varying degrees, almost every aspect of human behavior. The struggle by some activists to deny or downplay that fact is worrisome. The anti-gene claim is ultimately an ill-starred effort to preserve the myth that the environment can explain everything, and hence that political causes attempting to alter the environment can bring about whatever their leaders desire.

The truth is that though biology is not destiny, it may be a massive obstacle on the path to utopia.

15

The Future of Blame

Originally published in National Affairs, Winter 2010

If, as I argued in the previous essay, genes play a large role in determining how we behave, what does this mean for our ability to hold people personally accountable for their actions? My answer: not much.

A distinguished American lawyer once remarked that "man is in no sense the maker of himself and has no more power than any other machine to escape the law of cause and effect." The speaker was Clarence Darrow, who, eighty years ago, was trying to help Nathan Leopold and Richard Loeb escape the death penalty for having murdered Bobby Franks in cold blood. "Each act, criminal or otherwise, follows a cause," Darrow continued, and "given the same conditions the same result will follow forever and ever."

The argument that people are essentially machines has gained greater traction in our time, thanks in no small part to our improved scientific understanding of how genes shape our minds, and how our minds shape our behavior. We have long known that genes completely control the color of our eyes, help to determine our intelligence, and play a major role in the emergence of countless traits, conditions, and diseases. But of late we have also learned that genes heavily influence our personalities, our attitudes toward religion and morality, and even our political ideologies. Developments in neuroscience, meanwhile, have pointed to strong correlations between the structure of a person's brain and the character of his judgments and actions.

These developments raise questions that go to the heart of our moral and legal systems: Does the fact that biology determines more of our thinking and conduct than we had previously imagined undermine the notion of free will? And does this reality in turn undermine, if not destroy entirely, the possibility of holding people accountable for their actions? The answer to these questions must of course be informed by what science now tells us. But above all, it demands that we honestly reassess the assumptions underlying our society's systems of ethics and justice.

It turns out that those assumptions are far less vulnerable to advances in modern science than they might first appear. And therefore the answer to the question of accountability would appear to be the same today as it was when Clarence Darrow raised it eight decades ago: New advances do not render irrelevant or unjust our ways of holding people responsible for their behavior.

Explaining Behavior

No serious scientist claims that modern biology can now offer us a complete explanation of human behavior, or a foolproof code for predicting human judgments and actions. Our knowledge of our genes and our brains is just too limited. Duke University professor David Goldstein, a leading population geneticist, has noted that so far even the effort to find the genes that explain common diseases has borne very little fruit. We recognize that type 2 diabetes is heritable, but so far the genes known to be linked to it explain only 2 or 3 percent of the disparity in the odds of different people getting the disease. Harvard professor Steven Pinker recently wrote in the *New York Times Magazine* about having his own genome completely analyzed; among the lessons he learned is just how far we are from translating maps of genes into useful explanations or predictions regarding our bodily selves. Height, for example, is almost entirely inherited, but we do not understand the genetic mechanism by which it is inherited, and what we do know so far explains just 2 percent of the height differences among people. Intelligence, too, is largely inherited, but the gene with the biggest known effect on brain power usually accounts for only one-quarter of an IQ point. As Pinker observes, genes affect the probability that we will have some trait, but no one gene—or even a package of genes—simply explains the trait's existence.

Similarly, the study of the brain has offered some fascinating insight into the neurobiological correlates of certain behaviors, but it cannot at this point claim to offer anything approaching a predictive model of behavior. So while we are in a golden age of neuroscience—and while we certainly know far more about the brain and its workings than ever before—we are far from reducing human actions and choices to maps of neural activity.

Some argue that such explanatory power might in fact never be possible—either because some ephemeral, overarching element of human consciousness (call it a soul) cannot be reduced to the mere electrochemical processes of the brain, or because the full complexity of those processes will never be entirely accessible to science. But our approach to the question of modern biology and free will cannot begin by assuming that science will not get far enough to force the issue. We need to take seriously the possibility that it will. After all, fifty years ago, we had no idea what a gene looked like. Ten years ago, we had not unraveled a single human genome. Advances in neuroimaging over just the past two decades make the techniques of the 1980s seem primitive. There is every reason to expect continued progress, and it may well be the case that, over time, human behavior will prove far more accessible to scientific explanation than it appears today.

We can already begin to see the spheres of human action in which this possibility may first become a reality. Societies have long known, for instance, that young men commit far more crimes than other people do. Today we know that about 6 percent of all males cause between one-half and two-thirds of all violent crimes. Studies supporting this finding have been conducted in jurisdictions as far-flung as Denmark and New Zealand, as well as in Philadelphia, Racine (Wisconsin), and Orange County (California). Research also tells us that criminal males often have childhood conduct disorders, and that many are psychopathic—not merely violent but arrogant, deceitful, and lacking in any emotional attachment to others.

Given most people's experience, the fact that men—especially young men—are more violent than women would seem to be obvious. But in the present state of research, the relationship is actually just a statistical correlation. Suppose, however, that it were much more: that by tracing levels of hormones and neurotransmitters, science could show just why and how young men—and even which young men in particular—are far more prone to violence than other human beings.

We have good reasons for thinking that neuroscience will someday do just that. Dr. Louann Brizendine, a neuropsychiatrist at the University of California,

San Francisco, has summarized the evidence we have so far: The part of the brain that stimulates our anger and aggression (the amygdala) is much larger in men than in women, while the part of the brain that restrains anger (the prefrontal cortex) is smaller in men than in women. Newborn boys are much less interested in the cries of other babies than are newborn girls; very young boys are much more likely to disobey their mothers than are girls; and the testosterone in boys' brains makes them much more aggressive and less interested in talking or in social connections than (largely) testosterone-free girls. All the evidence points in one direction: men, by no choice of their own, are far more prone to violence and far less capable of self-restraint than women.

Given the apparent speed with which genetic analysis and neuroscience are advancing, it may be possible in the near future to explain aggressive or criminal behavior in far more detail still. We may be able to show, for instance, that particular men—as distinguished by neurologic or genetic traits—are especially prone to certain violent behaviors. Some neuroscientists think that, with time, such traits may even be used to explain behavior and judgment more generally. We already know that different areas of the brain "light up" (that is, acquire increased blood flow) as people judge moral questions; it may turn out that different people are powerfully predisposed by their neurobiology to different kinds of judgments. As Patricia Churchland of the University of California, San Diego, has put it: "As we understand more about the details of the regulatory systems in the brain and how decisions emerge in neural networks, it is increasingly evident that moral standards, practices, and policies reside in our neurobiology."

If this claim turns out to be true, how will it affect our judgment of free will? And what will become of our system of justice, grounded as it is in the notion of individual responsibility? Will understanding human behavior at the level of genetics and neurobiology make it unreasonable or impossible to hold people accountable for what they do?

The Social Animal

To deal with these questions, we must begin by acknowledging that our laws are meant to serve the needs of a society, not just of the individuals within it. As every philosopher since Aristotle has recognized, humans are social animals. What we do depends not only on who we are, but also on whom we know and to whom we respond.

In order to show people that no explanation of human behavior can neglect its social setting, Professor Stephen Morse of the University of Pennsylvania Law School often asks people who are hearing him speak to stand and raise one arm. Almost everyone does. He then asks them to lower their arms and be seated. They do. Assume, for the moment, that all of the audience's behavior has been explained by their genetic makeup or through scans of their brains. They still stand and sit when politely asked to do so. The explanation of human behavior, then, includes one person's reaction to another person's request. Their biology will have explained their social nature.

Understanding human behavior therefore requires that we understand not only how people are shaped by their genetic makeup, their acquired psychological experiences, and the manner in which their brains work, but also how they respond to the behavior of people around them. Very little human activity is driven exclusively by impulses from within the actor. A lone, sober juvenile rarely creates a threatening disturbance, but a group of juveniles often will. Many motorists drive faster than the speed limit, but few motorists will speed when they are being followed by a police car. Our natural predispositions always interact with our social environment and our systems of rules and norms.

A good illustration of how social and genetic factors interact to shape behavior can be found in the work of Duke University's Terrie Moffitt. In her study of a group of boys growing up in Dunedin, New Zealand, Moffitt has found that those children who had a certain variant of the monoamine oxidase A gene were much more likely to become antisocial if they had been severely maltreated by their parents. On the other hand, among boys who had the same version of the MAO-A gene but did not experience severe parental maltreatment, the level of antisocial behavior was much lower. It turns out that biology and environment interact; the boys' genetic makeup influences their responses to certain kinds of social pressures.

No serious explanation of human behavior, then, can ignore the social and cultural setting in which that behavior occurs. And since a society is far more than the sum of the individuals within it, no understanding of individual genes and brains—however sophisticated—can fully encompass all human behavior.

That our behavior is always shaped by the social environment in which it takes place—even when it is also influenced by genetic factors—is an important justification for a system of law grounded in personal accountability. After all, the law—and its attitude toward fault and responsibility—helps to shape the very social environment that interacts with our natural predispositions. An enormous amount of what we do in life is a response to what others ask or expect of us; by setting clear, strictly enforced standards of behavior agreed upon by all of society, the law can play an instructive role unmatched by almost any other social institution.

It therefore makes sense for the law to hold people accountable even for some actions that are clearly involuntary. A person driving a car who has a grand mal epileptic seizure will lose control of the vehicle and may well kill somebody. The law will take his condition into account in assigning fault, but this does not mean that the driver will bear no responsibility for his actions. The driver must take some blame—though he probably cannot be called a murderer—in order to make clear the value of the human lives he has destroyed. He must take even more blame if he knew that he had the disease (and almost everyone will know this long before applying for a driver's license) and drove anyway. In that case, the driver will generally be found guilty of reckless endangerment; he should have known better than to put himself in a position where his biological proclivities to certain behaviors could put others at risk. And one way the law helps him to know better is by setting out clear consequences for such actions.

Another way our system of assigning responsibility and blame takes account of human free will is by shaping how people think about what they do and do not want. Princeton philosopher Harry Frankfurt notes that while being moved by desires is not a uniquely willful or even a uniquely human trait, human beings are distinguished by having preferences about what they *ought* to desire—preferences that transform the relationship between behavior and responsibility.

Frankfurt offers an example. Imagine that there are three men, each equally addicted to dangerous drugs. The first desperately wishes he were not addicted and fights, unsuccessfully, to overcome his dependency.

The second does not mind being addicted and does nothing to overcome it. The third is delighted with his addiction and revels in it. All three are in a very similar biological state—a physical addiction. It may even be that their attitudes about that state are significantly determined by their biology, too. But these attitudes are not *completely* determined. We all know people who have radically changed their attitudes about their own self-destructive behavior. The degree to which people exhibit this desire for self-improvement is often highly relevant to how society will think of them—and therefore to how the law will judge them.

In Frankfurt's view, these three men have free will in the sense that each is "free to want what he wants to want." One man wants to overcome addiction, the second is content with it, and the third greatly enjoys it. Someday soon we may be able to explain the addiction through genetics and neuroscience, but do we think we can explain these differing attitudes in the same way? And if we could, should it make any difference to society at large?

The answer depends on one's view of the ultimate purpose of the law. If one believes that the criminal law should punish addiction because it is wrong, all three would be penalized. If one thinks the criminal law should attempt to deter addiction so that people will be encouraged to avoid it, all would still be punished, but the first man less seriously than the other two. If one's opinion is that we should rehabilitate offenders, then the first man would be required to enter a treatment program, while the other two would be sent to jail. And if one is of the mind that we should never punish addiction, we would take action against none of them.

The difference in our treatment of the three men may be influenced by our growing understanding of addiction as a physiological matter, but it will have far more to do with whether we think addiction creates problems for society. If the answer is yes, the next step is determining how the problem ought to be managed: by isolating addicts from everyone else (we call this incapacitation); discouraging others from becoming addicts (deterrence); changing a person's addiction level (rehabilitation); or expressing and reinforcing society's objections to addiction (retribution). The law can pursue any combination of these four different responses to the problem of addiction—but all of them represent views about how to shape choices and behavior, grounded in the understanding that attitude matters.

Just Punishment

Some people, perhaps influenced by our growing understanding of the biological determinants of behavior, believe that incapacitation, deterrence, and rehabilitation may be reasonable justifications for punishment, but that retribution never is. The first three, they argue, are efforts to protect individuals and society and can be defended on practical grounds: if the benefits to society exceed the costs, then we are helping law-abiding people by punishing or changing law-breaking people. Retribution, however, can only be an error: it is merely a denunciation of behavior. Punishing people on retributive grounds is of no practical value to society.

This view is, quite frankly, mistaken, and for reasons that remain undiminished by advances in our understanding of the biology of behavior. Consider the example of rape. Suppose neuroscience discovered a pill that, when swallowed, would reduce to zero the likelihood that a convicted rapist will ever rape again. We would still want to arrest rapists, of course, but once convicted, a rapist's only punishment would be the pill. In this scenario, the benefits to society would be great, and the cost would be rather small.

Except, that is, to a victim of rape. She would think that a violent attack on her person surely deserves a stronger penalty than swallowing a pill, and much of society would, too. The rapist must therefore be punished in order to achieve two goals: first, inflicting harm on the rapist that somehow corresponds to the harm the victim has suffered, and, second, reinforcing society's view that rape is wrong. In short, punishment for a serious crime should have a retributive component.

This is how most people tend to think about matters of crime and punishment. Scholars like to argue for or against a particular theory of punishment, but legislators, judges, and the public generally link the various justifications together. A punishment is fitting only if it incapacitates known offenders, deters would-be offenders, increases the chances of rehabilitating offenders, and expresses a solemn moral judgment about the wrongness of the criminal act. This commonly shared four-pronged approach to punishment is deeply grounded in a belief in free will and personal responsibility—and yet would not be significantly undermined by advances in biology that explain more of human behavior in genetic or neurological terms.

Society can, and should, still punish people even if neuroscience has fully explained their actions. We all know, and the common law clearly recognizes, that a person may not be guilty of a crime if he acted under duress; but we also know that there are limits to what duress can justify. You may be forced at gunpoint to drive a robber to a bank, but ordinarily you will not be held guilty of the robbery that ensues. On the other hand, if you were forced at gunpoint to deliberately kill an innocent person, you can be judged guilty of the killing. Duress is one of many factors a judge and jury would consider, not an all-encompassing excuse.

So too with biological predispositions. A young man loaded with testosterone, lacking interest in other people, and driven by impulses rather than reflection may find it much harder to avoid crime than a young woman who has little testosterone, is closely attached to others, and is shy about acting impulsively. To avoid criminal behavior, the male has to climb a steeper hill than the female. It may therefore seem unfair for the law to treat their behavior equally.

But it is actually the man who benefits more from a system of laws that attribute blame and responsibility. Because he must climb the steeper hill, he is in greater need of the incentive and guidance the law will provide. If the hill were made flat to save him from the unfair exertion—so that each person was expected to behave only as biology might direct—we would make life only superficially easier for our aggressive young man, and much harder for both the better-behaved woman and for society more broadly. For if we allow ourselves to think that explaining behavior justifies it, then we will have reduced the incentives for people who are likely to behave wrongly to avoid that behavior. We will also have reduced the likelihood that people behaving well will recognize that they are doing the right things.

This final point is vital. A system of laws rooted in the assumption of personal responsibility and accountability helps us define not only bad behavior but also good. If we believe modern science has explained wrongful behavior, we must also argue that it has explained praiseworthy behavior. Virtue then becomes just as meaningless as depravity—a state of affairs in which no society could hope to remain ordered or healthy.

Praise and Blame

As the late Isaiah Berlin put it, scientific determinism would render both indignation and admiration irrational and obsolete. Were we to withhold our disapproval of criminals, we would have to stifle the praise we give to heroes. If science tells us why Charles Manson or Lyle Menendez acted as they did, it will also tell us why Nelson Mandela or Mother Teresa acted as they did— and will in fact suggest that they could hardly have done otherwise.

However far science may go toward explaining the behavior of individuals, it will not make will, fault, and choice irrelevant to society. To accept the proposition that determinism is a higher road to justice and fairness would lead us into an empty world, one devoid not only of transgression, but also of virtue, forgiveness, and redemption. As Berlin put it, "the entire vocabulary of human relations would suffer radical change." It might well be the most profound change in human thinking since mankind first began to contemplate the meaning of our conduct. If we can neither blame nor praise, then the concepts of personal morality and human freedom will be lost, and with them much of what they have gained for us over several millennia.

It would be a profound mistake to believe that science has made such a change unavoidable. For all the advances in neurobiology and genetics— and for all the many sure to come—we are nowhere near a refutation of the basic truth or fairness of a system of laws that takes free will seriously, and treats human beings as responsible agents. Those who believe such a change is at hand are not better informed about the science involved; they are not informed enough about the practical and philosophical foundations of our morality and justice.

Conclusion
America versus the World

How the world views the United States has recently undergone a profound change. In 2007 the Pew Global Attitudes Project asked people in many countries whether they had a favorable or unfavorable attitude toward this country and whether they had confidence or no confidence in the American president. The table below shows results for two groups of nations: our allies and key Muslim nations.

ATTITUDES TOWARD THE UNITED STATES AND THE U.S. PRESIDENT,
U.S. ALLIES VERSUS KEY MUSLIM NATIONS

	Favorable view of the United States		Confidence in the U.S. President	
	2007	2009	2007	2009
Britain	52%	69%	24%	86%
Canada	55	68	28	88
France	39	75	14	91
Germany	30	64	19	93
Japan	61	59	35	85
Poland	61	67	29	62
Egypt	21	27	8	42
Jordan	20	25	8	31
Pakistan	15	16	7	13
Palestine	13	15	8	23
Turkey	9	14	2	33

SOURCE: Pew Global Attitudes Project.

The change is remarkable. Support for our country rose dramatically in Britain, Canada, France, and Germany; indeed, in the last two nations it more than doubled. (It remained favorable but essentially unchanged in Japan and Poland.) In the Muslim world, by contrast, there was hardly any improvement at all. In Egypt, Jordan, Pakistan, the Palestinian territories, and Turkey, this country remains very unpopular.

Much of the improvement can be explained by Barack Obama being our president. George W. Bush was deeply unpopular everywhere in the world in 2007, whereas Obama had achieved rock star status in Canada, Europe, and Japan. He holds the confidence of 93 percent of all Germans and 91 percent of the French. I find it hard to believe that this fraction of Germans and French agree on anything else.

Obama is also more popular than Bush in Egypt and Jordan, but most people in these countries still dislike the president. Our president has gone to great lengths to attract Muslim support, and while he has made gains among Muslims, he remains more popular among our allies. If the president's goal was to restore American prestige among Muslims, he has made some but not much progress. Over 40 percent of Egyptians say they like him, but only 27 percent have a favorable view of this country.

What is really important is not the standing of the president but the profound differences between this country and the rest of the world. As I explained earlier in this book, our political and religious traditions have made us the opposite of most of the Muslim world. We value personal freedom and support religious faiths that have no room for jihad or terrorism. No presidential speech in Cairo can change that. What can lessen the difference between America and the Muslim world is slow progress in Muslim nations of the sort we have seen in Indonesia and a few other places. This country can help but it cannot export or direct those changes.

And we differ as well from our allies. In many key aspects of our lives we have views that are very different from theirs. Return to the Pew Global Attitudes Project. Over 70 percent of Americans are very proud to be a part of this nation, more than twice the fraction of Western Europeans who are proud to be part of their countries. Well over half (58 percent) of Americans prefer personal freedom to a government safety net, but 60 percent of Europeans prefer the safety net to individual freedom. One third of Americans believe our fate is determined by outside forces, not personal behavior, while nearly two-thirds of Europeans think it is "outside control" and not one's own conduct that shapes their fate.

In the book we coedited, Peter H. Schuck and I defended the idea of American exceptionalism.[1] America is the most religious of all economically developed nations. Over 40 percent of Americans go to a church, synagogue, or mosque every week; only 5 percent of the French do the same. To some this is a striking fact inasmuch as in France and all of Europe religion was once supported and paid for by the state.

But it is because religion once had state support that it became weaker. Elsewhere in this book I have shown that when the state supports a church, the church suffers if the state suffers. When you fight or vote against a government you are often fighting and voting against the church the state endorses. When you leave religion to individuals and ban any state-supported church, as our Bill of Rights does, religion spreads by the competitive activities of preachers, priests, rabbis, and imams. Religion prospers precisely because it lacks state support.

American exceptionalism can be seen in every aspect of our lives. We have a limited government based on natural rights, not divine sanction, monarchical tradition, or a supreme parliament. When the government here tries to do too much, the people organize "tea parties" to protest these changes. By contrast, when the French government does too little, angry Frenchmen mount a strike and block the roads in and out of Paris.

Despite a history of discrimination and barriers, America has done better at integrating its ethnic groups than most European nations. There are several million Muslims living here, but despite the role of jihadists in attacking the World Trade Center and a growth in American suspicion of some Muslim groups, American Muslims earn more money than the national average and hold important positions in every walk of life.

America is the most generous of all nations. This is in part due to the religious background of Americans, but as Arthur Brooks has pointed out, religious Americans give more money to secular causes than do secular Americans.[2] Not only do Americans do more than private persons in other countries to help the disadvantaged, we put in place an extraordinary variety of private institutions—universities, hospitals, think tanks—that not only provide help but also support a variety of opinions that enrich public discourse.

American exceptionalism has costs as well as benefits. We were slow to put in place the necessary features of a welfare system that can help people cope with unemployment and personal crises. Our adversarial legal system entangles many of us in pointless and costly disputations. Our public schools often fail to prepare people for either work or citizenship. We have to overcome the legacy of racism.

But Americans seem to want these problems addressed in, well, an American way. When President Obama proposed an elaborate, costly, and rule-driven health care system, it stalled in Congress in part because too many voters either could not understand it or did not want it. The tea party movement has been driven by a popular fear of rapidly rising deficits; that effort has meant that Moveon.org has met its match, and so the ideological struggle in this country now has strong groups on both sides.

And it is an ideological struggle. The Left wishes America to become a European-style social democracy, the Right wishes it to remain a nation with a limited government and a reasonably free economy. In my view, the Left is wrong, but I do not doubt for a moment the seriousness of the efforts it is making. To me, American exceptionalism is vital, not only for our citizens but for the countless people in Bosnia, Iraq, Israel, Kuwait, Taiwan, and elsewhere whom we have helped without asking anything in return. We cannot be the policeman of the world, but we can fight back against the worst forms of tyranny even when (perhaps especially when) our allies will not.

Notes

1. Peter H. Schuck and James Q. Wilson, eds., *Understanding America: The Anatomy of an Exceptional Nation* (New York: Public Affairs Press, 2008), chap. 21.

2. Arthur C. Brooks, *Who Really Cares? America's Charity Divide* (New York: Basic Books, 2006), 34–35.

Index

Tulluck, Gordon, 36
Turkey, 151, 155, 156–57
Twin research and personality power
    of genetics, 178–80

United Kingdom, *See* England
United States
    American exceptionalism, xiv, 195–96
    other countries' views of, 193–94
    religion's role in, 98–99, 102–4, 195
    voluntary association in, 45, 72–78
    See also American politics

Vadakian, James C., 36
Verba, Sidney, 14
Veto-group politics, 16
Victorian self-control vs. modern
    self-expression, 46
Vietnam War, 53–59, 63, 82, 83, 84
Virtue, private, and public policy, 35–49
    See also Moral judgment
Voluntary association in America, 45,
    72–78
Voters and voting
    congressional voting blocs,
        weakening of, 10
    genetic component to voting
        patterns, 178–79, 181
    identifying religious voters, 111–13
    ideological polarization, 66
    and polarization's complexities, 82
Vouchers, school, 33, 36

Wahid, Abdurrahman (Gus Dur), 158
Wallace, George, 92

War coverage by media, biases in, 50–61
War party, 66
Warrantless wiretapping, 51–52
Weather Underground, 140
Weathermen, 133
Weber, Max, 43
Wedgwood, C. V., 146
Welfare programs, effect on character
    and public policy, 39–42
Western societies
    democracy development, 155, 165–73
    individualism in, 152, 167
    reconciliation of freedom and religion
        in, 143–53
    See also American politics; Europe
White, William, 11
Wildavsky, Aaron, 36
Will, George F., 155
Williams, Roger, 147
Wilson, A. N., 128
Wilson, James Q., 78
Wilson-Patterson Scale, 178
Wiretapping, warrantless, 51–52
Wolfe, Alan, 115, 117
Women as suicide terrorists, 135
World War II, xii, 52–53
Wright, James D., 55
Wuthnow, Robert, 110

Yassine, Abdessalam, 162
Yudhoyno, Susilio Bambang, 158

Zaller, John R., 88–89
Zionism, Christian participation in,
    125–26

About the Author

James Q. Wilson lectures at Pepperdine University and Boston College and was previously a professor of government at Harvard and a professor of management and public policy at UCLA. He is the author of several books, including *Bureaucracy: What Government Agencies Do and Why They Do It* (Basic Books, 1991), *On Character* (AEI Press, 1995), *Political Organizations* (Princeton University Press, 1995), *The Moral Sense* (Free Press, 1997), and *The Marriage Problem: How Our Culture Has Weakened Families* (Harper, 2003). A new book, co-edited with Joan Petersilia, *Crime and Public Policy*, is forthcoming from Oxford University Press. Wilson was awarded the Presidential Medal of Freedom by President George W. Bush and received the Bradley Prize from the Bradley Foundation. He is the chairman of the Council of Academic Advisers of the American Enterprise Institute.